Women
And
Business Ownership
A Bibliography

Edited By
Marcia LaSota

Minnesota Scholarly Press, Inc.

Minnesota Scholarly Press, Inc.
P.O. Box 224
Mankato, MN 56001
$ 37.50

ISBN 0-933474-45-8

Table of Contents

APPENDICES

Preface

The phenomenon of women's involvement in business ownership has assumed a high profile over the past decade. During the 1970's women surged in unprecedented numbers into the labor force. In the 1980's women have increasingly chosen business ownership as a career option.

The 1985 State of Small Business report identifies women's businesses as "the fastest growing segment of the small business population[1];" and points out that women's businesses are now firmly ensconced in the mainstream of economic growth -- the burgeoning service sector, which is increasingly described as the "new entrepreneurial economy." This bibliography documents the state-of-the-art in describing this energetic new economic phenomenon.

Everything that has been written about women's businesses or the woman as entrepreneur over the past several years has not been included here, however. The intent has been, rather, to select those writings and information which may be of greatest interest to researchers and policy and program developers. Listed and discussed herein are formal research documents, unpublished dissertations and theses, charts and tables, unpublished government reports, government hearing records, legal case books, selected articles and books from the popular press, and popular guides to small business management for women.

As is usually the case with bibliographies, the picture offered will be incomplete even on the day it is published, for new publications appear daily, and references included and critiqued here have been subject to editorial judgment. Since this is the first such compendium, it is hoped that the cited references, and the perspectives offered on them will encourage further investigation of this new phenomenon. As will be seen, a more focused and scientific approach is needed as well as improvements in data sources without which more focused and scientific studies will be impossible.

---

[1]The State of Small Business: A Report of the President, (Washington, D.C.: U.S. Government Printing Office, May 1985).

Section I:
Introduction

During the 1980's women business owners have increased their visibility as important contributors to the vitality of the U.S. economy. Women-owned businesses now represent the fastest-growing segment of the small business sector. While the total number of businesses owned by women is still small when compared to the number of businesses owned by men, the rate of increase of women choosing self-employment is several times the corresponding figure for men.[2] In 1983, 27.6 percent of all sole proprietorships were female operated, up from 22.6 percent in 1977.[3] In 1985, the Small Business Administration estimated that there were three million women-owned non-farm businesses, including partnerships and corporations, as well as sole proprietorships.[4]

As the number of businesses owned by women has increased, the organized constituency has become more visible and business ownership for women has attracted more attention as a field of research and public policy development. Since the mid 1970's, a number of popular small business guides targeted to present and potential women business owners have appeared, Congressional hearings have been held, a federal policy elaborated, organizations formed, and research conducted, sponsored both by the Federal Government and by the private sector.

Nevertheless, there are still no more than a handful of well-structured, scholarly studies directly related to women's business ownership. The existing body of research has been difficult to access because many of the studies are unpublished or have appeared in scholarly journals which do not receive wide circulation. This introductory essay is not intended to give a full description or analysis of the major writings on women's business ownership --there are summaries of these in the bibliographic entries that follow. Here we will attempt to describe the scope and extent of the literature, examine emerging issues in the field and provide background information that may make the bibliography more useful.

In this introduction, we will examine the reliability and availability of data on women business owners and their firms; the findings of the most significant research to date on women business owners as well as the shortcomings of that research; barriers to business ownership for women; and, finally, government efforts on behalf of present and potential women business owners--a subject which has generated many noteworthy reports, hearing records and other assessments.

---

[2]U.S. Department of Labor, Bureau of Labor Statistics, Employment and Earnings (Washington, D.C: various years).

[3]U.S. Department of the Treasury, Internal Revenue Service, Statistics of Income: Sole Proprietorships Returns. (Washington, D.C., 1985).

[4]U.S. Small Business Administration, The State of Small Business, (Washington, D.C.: U.S. Government Printing Office, 1985), 298.

Data Limitations

The publication of the first census[5] of women-owned businesses in 1976 stimulated development of a large body of popular articles and scholarly papers that reviewed the census findings and raised research questions. The ability to pursue lines of inquiry on questions raised by this early work has been limited by a persisting lack of comparable, timely and regularly available data. Most of the sources of information on U.S. businesses still do not identify either the gender or the racial/ethnic origin of the business owner. The census of women-owned businesses is only published every five years (with a four-year lag), and other official data sources on women business owners and their firms do not count the owners or their firms in the same fashion as does the U.S. Census Bureau.

There are four main sources of data on women-owned businesses that are readily available to the public. They are: the census of women-owned business (1972 and 1977 are now available; 1982 will be released in 1986); the Statistics of Income for Sole Proprietorships published by the Internal Revenue Service (IRS) (information available by gender of owner for the tax years 1977, 1979, 1980, 1982 and 1983); the statistics on self-employed individuals published by the Bureau of Labor Statistics (BLS) in the monthly publication, Employment and Earnings; and the current population reports.

Unfortunately, the figures reported by these sources are not consistent with each other. For example, in 1977 (the only year for which data from all these sources are available), according to the IRS, there were 1,900,723 female-operated sole proprietorships in non-farm industries. The census of women-owned businesses for that same year put the number at only 701,957, including 532,000 sole-proprietorships.[6] The discrepancy between the IRS and census figures exists despite the fact that the primary source of data for the 1977 census was the IRS.

More recent statistics, while they differ, indicate that the 1972 census figure is probably underestimated. The 1983 IRS statistics of income report 3,254,000 female-operated non-farm sole proprietorships, representing 27.6 percent of all such businesses.[7] BLS reports that women were 33.4 percent of the 7,811,000 non-farm self-employed Americans in 1985.[8] Finally, the

---

[5]U.S. Department of Commerce, Bureau of the Census, Women-Owned Businesses, 1972, (Washington, D.C.: U.S. Government Printing Office, 1976).

[6]Ibid., 7-8.

[7]U.S. Department of the Treasury, Internal Revenue Service, Statistics of Income: Sole Proprietorship Returns, 1985, (Washington, D.C.: U.S. Government Printing Office, 1985),.

[8]U.S. Department of Labor, Bureau of Labor Statistics, Employment and Earnings, January, 1986 (unpublished at press time).

Small Business Administration, using data from the Internal Revenue Service has estimated that there were some three million women-owned businesses in 1984.[9]

Another problem encountered in determining an accurate count of women-owned firms is the fact that different definitions of "woman-owned" are used. The U.S. Small Business Administration's Office of Women's Business Ownership defines a woman-owned business as one that is at least 51 percent owned, operated and controlled by a woman or women (this includes control of operations on a day-to-day basis).[10] The Census Bureau considers a business to be women-owned if the sole owner or half or more of the partners are women, or, in a corporation, if 50 percent or more of the stock is owned by women.[11] Meanwhile, the Internal Revenue Service estimates the number of "female-operated" firms only for sole proprietorships--by using the first names from the Form 1040, Schedule C that must be filed by business owners.[12] The IRS does not collect or analyze data by sex on partnerships or corporations. (A recent survey by the National Association of Women Business Owners (NAWBO) suggests that this is a serious omission. In a recent survey of its membership it was reported that 47 percent of the firms owned by NAWBO members responding were corporations, suggesting that the economic profile of the organized constituency is very different from the profile emerging from self-employed and sole-proprietorship data.[13]) Finally, the Bureau of Labor Statistics (BLS) figures count only the number of people reporting to be self employed, not the number of businesses they own nor their share of ownership.[14] The BLS figures also do not capture all U.S. business owners. Corporate owners and partners are excluded from the count, since BLS counts these individuals separately as wage and salary workers. In addition, individuals who are self-employed in a second job, but work for someone else in their primary job are not included in the count.

---

[9]U.S. Small Business Administration, State of Small Business, 1985, 298.

[10]President's Interagency Task Force on Women Business Owners, The Bottom Line: Unequal Enterprise in America, (U.S. Government Printing Office, 1978), 11ff.

[11]Bureau of the Census, Women-Owned Businesses, 1977, 4.

[12]U.S. Department of Treasury, Internal Revenue Service, Sole Proprietorship Returns, 1979-1980, (Washington, D.C.: U.S. Government Printing Office, 1982), 5-8.

[13]National Association of Women Business Owners, "NAWBO Membership Profile," (Chicago, National Association of Women Business Owners, 1984).

[14]Recent information on self-employed workers is analyzed in T. Scott Fain, "Self-Employed Americans: Their Number Has Increased," Monthly Labor Review (Nov. 1980): 3-8 and Eugene H. Becker, "Self-Employed Workers: An Update to 1983" Monthly Labor Review, 107, 7 (July, 1984): 14-18.

Despite problems with the data, the profiles of women-owned businesses as reported from all the principal federal government sources are remarkably compatible: all suggest that the typical woman-owned firm is a very small, service or retail concern with low receipts and few employees.

According to the latest economic census on women-owned businesses (1977), only 0.3 percent of all women-owned businesses have more than 100 employees, and 76 percent have no employees.[15] The 1977 census also reports that women-owned businesses are concentrated in the services and retail trade sectors (75 percent of all women-owned businesses were found to be concentrated in these two industrial categories).[16] Economic characteristics found in more recent reports from the Internal Revenue Service and the Bureau of Labor Statistics show that nearly 80% of all female-operated sole proprietorships were in retail trade and services in 1982,[17] while BLS reported that 86% of all self-employed women were working in those two categories in 1981.[18] In contrast, during these same periods, only 41 percent of male-operated sole proprietorships and 42 percent of self-employed men were in retail and services.[19]

The persistent concentration of women-owned firms in services and retail, along with their small size, may help to explain the low level of gross receipts and net income of women-owned firms relative to men-owned firms. IRS data on sole proprietorships reveal that, in 1980, female-operated sole proprietorships had an average net income equal to only 41 percent of the corresponding figure for male-operated firms in that category.[20] In that same year, year-round full-time self-employed women earned only 45.4 percent of the average earnings for male workers in the same class, according to the Bureau of Labor Statistics.[21]

A few authors whose works were reviewed in connection with the development of this bibliography have argued that many of the problems women business owners report, including perceived discrimination, may be related more to the types

---

[15]Bureau of the Census, Women-Owned Businesses, 1977, 8.

[16]Ibid., 12.

[17]IRS, Statistics of Income, 1982. Table 13, 192-195.

[18]BLS, Employment and Earnings (January, 1986).

[19]Ibid.

[20]IRS, Statistics of Income, 1982, table 13, 192-195.

[21]Bureau of Labor Statistics, Monthly Income of Households, Families, and Persons in the United States: 1980, Current Population Report: Consumer Income, p. 60 ser., 132, table 58 (Washington, D.C.: U.S. Department of Labor, 1982).

and sizes of businesses operated than to the fact that the owners are women.[22] If such is the case, the question then becomes: why are so many women entering low revenue, low growth, service and retail sales businesses? As we shall see, some researchers have attempted to answer this question in their discussions of the barriers to entrepreneurship for women.

Women as Entrepreneurs

Most studies have examined the personal characteristics of women business owners, rather than the economic profile of their businesses. Studies of women entrepreneurs have investigated questions similar to those raised about men entrepreneurs--especially the social and psychological determinants of entrepreneurship including motivation, personal values (including attitudes toward risk and achievement), and family and educational background.

Description of the fundamental role of entrepreneurship in the process of economic growth and development can be traced back to early classical economists Cantillon, Say, and Smith, but more recently to the influential work of Schumpeter.[23] The key element in Schumpeter's definition of entrepreneurship is innovation--the creation of new businesses, new products and new techniques of production, or what Schumpeter called "new combinations." Entrepreneurship is also characterized by risk taking. An individual who is capable of evaluating risks and is willing to make decisions in the face of considerable uncertainty, who takes initiative, identifies market needs, and brings together and organizes resources to meet those needs is labeled an entrepreneur.

Definitions of what constitutes entrepreneurship are still subject to debate today, forty years after Schumpeter. The phenomenon is defined alternatively in economic terms, in sociological terms, in terms of technical change, or in terms of a certain psychological profile (see Figure I). Some experts in the field of entrepreneurship studies make a distinction between the entrepreneur per se and the small business owner. Some definitions include all independent business owners; and some include upper-level managers of large

---

[22]This argument is explored at greater length below. Among those who raise this point, the following stand out: Ruth Finney, Toward a Typology of Women Entrepreneurs: Their Business Ventures and Family Life (Honolulu: East-West Center, 1977); Robert Hisrich and Marie O'Brien, "The Woman Entrepreneur as a Reflection of the Type of Business," Proceedings, 1982 Conference on Entrepreneurship (Boston: Babson College, 1982); Patricia McNamara, "Business Ownership: A New Career Option for Women," New Directions for Education, Work and Careers, no. 8 (1979): 71-82.

[23]Joseph A. Schumpeter, Capitalism, Socialism and Democracy (New York: Harper and Rowe, Publishers, 1942).

corporations or extend the concept of entrepreneurship to the socialist economy.[24] In much of the literature on women business owners, as in common parlance, entrepreneur as a descriptive term is often utilized as a synonym for the successful independent business person--one who risks his or her personal assets and shares any future monetary gain associated with a venture.

For the purpose of this review we will follow the common practice of the researchers whose work is reviewed here, using a broad definition of the entrepreneur as one who takes an active role in the decision making and risk taking of a business in which s/he has majority ownership.

A fundamental debate in the field of entrepreneurship studies concerns the question of whether entrepreneurship should be identified with a specific event or action that constitutes the actualization of the entrepreneurial function (new venture formation) or with the individuals who set such events in motion.[25] The bulk of the literature shows a partiality to the latter. Thus, the motivation for new venture creation, or those factors that promote or encourage new ventures, are most frequently discussed with reference to the personal and psychological characteristics of the enterprising individual. Probably the most well-known in this area is McClelland's seminal work, The Achieving Society, in which McClelland posits that the need for achievement is the key factor prompting people to start businesses.[26]

Socially-sanctioned sex role stereotyping has encouraged female achievement to be viewed almost exclusively in terms of supportive or dependent roles such as homemaker and mother. In contrast, a man's success is universally judged by the degree of his economic achievement. Because of this dichotomy in society's view of male and female achievement, there may be a tendency for observers who are influenced by McClelland to describe women as socially disadvantaged with respect to entrepreneurship.[27] These commentators see prevailing socialization of women and the personality traits resulting from this socialization process as major barriers to successful entrepreneurship among women.

Because nearly all studies of entrepreneurs have focused on men exclusively, one research question that must be addressed is the extent to which women can

---

[24]Calvin Kent, Donald Sexton and Karl Vesper, eds., Encyclopedia of Entrepreneurship (Englewood Cliffs, N.J.: Prentice-Hall, 1982) contains a great deal of discussion on just this point, offering a number of different definitions of entrepreneurship.

[25]Albert Shapero and Lisa Sokol, "Social Dimensions of Entrepreneurship," in Encyclopedia of Entrepreneurship, ed. Kent, Sexton, and Vesper, 72-90.

[26]David C. McClelland, The Achieving Society, (Princeton, N.J.: D. Van Nostrand Co., Inc., 1961).

[27]This view is explained in Eleanor Schwartz, "Entrepreneurship: A New Female Frontier," Journal of Contemporary Business (Winter 1976): 47-76.

Figure I: Key Entrepreneurial Characteristics

- Self-confidence

- Perseverance, determination

- Energy, diligence

- Resourcefulness

- Ability to take calculated risks

- Need to achieve

- Creativity

- Initiative

- Flexibility

- Positive response to challenges

- Independence

- Foresight

- Dynamism, leadership

- Versatility, knowledge of product, market, machinery, technology

- Ability to get along with people

- Responsiveness to suggestions and criticism

- Profit-orientation

- Perceptiveness

- Optimism

Source: Calvin Kent, Donald Sexton and Karl Vesper, eds., Encyclopedia of Entrepreneurship (Englewood Cliffs, N.J.: Prentice-Hall, 1982), 28.

be compared with an entrepreneurial profile which has been developed through observations about men. Defining the woman entrepreneur becomes an important issue in itself. Studies conducted by Schwartz, Schreier, and the President's Interagency Task Force on Women Business Owners have focused heavily on developing a profile of the woman entrepreneur.[28] Figure 2 lists some of the common elements included in these "profiles."

Some studies compared their findings on women business owners to the results of separate studies on male entrepreneurs, concluding that there was little difference between the two groups. Only Welsch and Young actually used a sample of both male and female entrepreneurs.[29] Others used a female sample and then compared their findings to the results of previous research, including a 1971 study of male entrepreneurs conducted by Hornaday and Aboud.[30] Hornaday and Aboud had compared the personal values of successful male business owners with those of the general populace and found that entrepreneurs scored much higher on the scales reflecting need for achievement, independence and effectiveness of leadership.[31]

The picture that emerges from these studies is one in which the female entrepreneur is very much like her male counterpart, at least in terms of psychological traits. Sexton and Kent also found few differences between women entrepreneurs and women managers while earlier research had shown significant differences between male business owners and managers.[32] DeCarlo and Lyons

---

[28]Ibid.; See also James Schreier, The Female Entrepreneur: A Pilot Study (Milwaukee: Center for Venture Management, 1975); Interagency Task Force, The Bottom Line.

[29]Harold Welsch and Earl Young, "Comparative Analysis of Male and Female Entrepreneurs with Respect to Personality Characteristics, Small Business Problems, and Information Source Preferences" (Chicago: DePaul University, 1982, mimeographed); Earl Young and Harold Welsch, "Differences Between Male and Female Entrepreneurs with Respect to Personality Characteristics Relating to Information Search Behavior" (Chicago: DePaul University, 1982, mimeographed).

[30]James DeCarlo and Paul Lyons, "A Comparison of Selected Personal Characteristics of Minority and Non-Minority Female Entrepreneurs," Journal of Small Business Management 17 (October 1979): 22-29. James DeCarlo and Paul Lyons, "Characteristics of Successful Female Entrepreneurs" (Frostburg, MD: Frostburg State College, 1978, mimeographed); Norman Smith, Gary McCain, and Audrey Warren, "Women Entrepreneurs Really Are Different," Frontiers of Entrepreneurship Research 1982 (Boston: Babson College, 1982); See also Schwartz, "A New Female Frontier" and Schreier, The Female Entrepreneur.

[31]John Hornaday and John Aboud, "Characteristics of Successful Entrepreneurs," Personnel Psychology 24 (Summer 1971).

[32]Donald Sexton and Calvin Kent, "Female Executives and Entrepreneurs: A Preliminary Comparison" (Waco, TX: Baylor University, 1981, mimeographed); H. Hartman, "Managers and Entrepreneurs: A Useful Distinction" Administration Science Quarterly 3 (March 1959): 429-451.

Figure II: Profile of the Woman Entrepreneur

- operates a relatively new, young firm--her first entrepreneurial effort

- founder of her business

- few employees

- owns a service or retail business

- used personal savings or assets as the primary source of start-up finance

- between 35 and 55 years old

- formerly married, or still married, with a family

- more highly educated than the national average

- immediate family members are also self-employed-- parents and/or siblings

- motivated by a desire for money, independence, and a chance to use her skills and talents

- employed for several years before starting her own business

- had work experience related to her current field of business (many had managerial experience).

Sources: President's Interagency Task Force on Women Business Owners, The Bottom Line: UnEqual Enterprise in America, (U.S. Government Printing Office), 1978; James Schreier, The Female Entrepreneur: A Pilot Study, (Milwaukee: Center for Venture Management, 1975); Eleanor Schwartz, "Entreneurship: A New Female Frontier," Journal of Contemporary Business, (Winter, 1976).

also studied managerial women and found almost no differences between them and women who owned and operated their own firms.[33] Meanwhile, Waddell, who compared women business owners, managers and secretaries, found that the combination of variables measuring achievement motivation, locus of control internality and sex role masculinity significantly discriminated among these three occupational groups;[34] and Carsrud, et. al., in a recent study comparing recent women MBA graduates with successful women business owners, found significant differences between the two groups.[35]

In studies conducted by the American Management Association[36], Schreier, Schwartz, DeCarlo and Lyons, Sexton and Kent, and Welsch and Young all uncovered few or no differences in experience, education and personality characteristics between women and men entrepreneurs. The two groups were found to be fairly similar with respect to many demographic characteristics and personality traits, including: family background--being the oldest and coming from an entrepreneurial family were important for both men and women; motivation for starting a business--need to achieve, desire for independence, economic necessity, new ideas, seizing an opportunity; psychological characteristics--achievement motivation, risk-taking propensity, leadership, independence, self-esteem, internal locus of control/feeling of control over own destiny; displacement--divorce, migration, unemployment, death of family member(s); previous work experience in business management or in a field related to the field of business.

Some differences were found in education--the level of education for women entrepreneurs was higher or lower than that of men, depending on the survey; and in attitude toward working for others--generally more positive for women than for men.

A recent study by Evans utilizing data from the Census Bureau's one percent Public Use Sample found that a smaller proportion of self-employed women (16.4 percent in 1980) than self-employed men (23.8 percent in 1980) were college-educated. The average age of self-employed women was higher than the average age of self employed men. Women who were self-employed also tended to have less education than women who were wage and salary workers. Statistical tests showed that for self-employed men there was a strong positive

---

[33]James DeCarlo and Paul Lyons, "An Exploratory Analysis of Job and Life Satisfaction Among Entrepreneurs," (Frostburg, MD: Frostburg State College, n.d., mimeographed).

[34]Frederick Thomass Waddell, "Factors Affecting Choice, Satisfaction and Success in the Female Self-Employed," (Ph. D. Dissertation, Ohio State University, 1982).

[35]Alan L. Carsrud, K. Olm and R. Ahegren, "Some Observations on Female Entrepreneurs and Female MBA Students," Working paper #84/85-4-32 (Austin, TX: University of Texas, 1984).

[36]Henry Bender, Report on Women Business Owners, (New York: American Management Association, June 1978).

relationship between earnings and education, but for self-employed women the relationship was not statistically significant.[37]

According to the Bureau of the Census,[38] information now nearly 10 years old, minority women constituted only about 6 percent of all women business owners. Preliminary research on minority women as business owners has been conducted by DeCarlo and Lyons, Lornes, and the National Business League. DeCarlo and Lyons found that the minority and non-minority women business owners surveyed differed with respect to personal characteristics and values as measured by certain psychological tests. The authors claimed their tests showed non-minority women entrepreneurs put a higher value on achievement, support, recognition and independence, while minority women placed a higher value on conformity and benevolence.[39]

Hisrich's study of women business owners in Puerto Rico found that in personal and educational characteristics, island-based Puerto Rican women entrepreneurs were very similar to U.S.- mainland women entrepreneurs surveyed as part of another study. However, the Puerto Rican women's businesses were more heavily concentrated in traditional "women's" fields.[40]

The report by the National Business League tends to confirm the picture of the black female entrepreneur elaborated by DeCarlo and Lyons,[41] while Lornes' work focuses on the characteristics of young black women who may want to become owners.[42] Both make recommendations for special training and other forms of assistance to aid minority women who want to start their own businesses. They echo the arguments made over the years in Congressional testimony -- that minority women in business face a double burden of

---

[37]David S. Evans, "Entrepreneurial Choice and Success," a study prepared for the Office of Veteran's Affairs, U.S. Small Business Administration (Greenwich, CT: CERA Economic Consultants, Inc., 1985).

[38]U.S. Department of Commerce, Bureau of the Census, Selected Characteristics of Women-Owned Businesses, 1977 (Washington D.C.: U.S. Government Printing Office, 1982).

[39]DeCarlo and Lyons, "A Comparison of Selected Characteristics...".

[40]Robert D. Hisrich, "The Women Entrepreneur in the United States and Puerto Rico: A Comparative Study," Leadership and Organization Development Journal 5, 5 (1984): 3-8.

[41]National Business League, Minority Women in Business (Washington, D.C., 1981).

[42]Millicent Lornes, "A Study of the Existence of Selected Characteristics that May Be Necessary for Entrepreneurial Success Among Black Female College Students Majoring in Business," (Ph.D. diss., Vanderbilt University, 1981).

institutional discrimination against women and against minorities.[43]. More research is needed in this area to determine the extent and implications of the "double burden" as it relates specifically to minority women's business ownership as well as how it can be overcome.

Research Problems

Researchers attempting to study women's business ownership have few ready sources for sampling that would permit hypothesis testing. The National Longitudinal Surveys, which provide 15 years of data on 4 cohorts of men and women contain too few observations on the self-employed to allow for meaningful statistical analysis. The Census Bureau's one percent Public Use Sample contains sufficient cases of self-employed individuals, but does not allow for year-to-year comparisons. As a result, most studies of women-owned businesses have had to collect their own data through mail or telephone surveys.

With the notable exceptions of the Census Bureau's Selected Characteristics of Women Business Owners, the survey by the President's Task Force on Women Business Owners, and that of the American Management Association, nearly all of the samples employed in the studies listed in this bibliography were drawn from general business directories or from directories of women-owned businesses, which results in considerable self-selection. In addition, these lists and directories are compiled in different ways depending on location. Some are made up almost entirely of businesses that have contacted state agencies for assistance. Thus, while these studies provide an interesting glimpse of the female entrepreneur, their findings and conclusions can not be generalized to the population of women business owners as a whole.

In an effort to improve the reliability of survey results, the U.S. Small Business Administration has attempted to estimate the proportions of male-operated, female-operated and joint male-female operated businesses in its Small Business Data Base (SBDB). Utilizing a sample of 224,588 businesses from the 8.1 million establishments in the SBDB Master Establishment List (MEL) file, the SBA's Office of Economic Research conducted a survey of ownership characteristics of those businesses. Based on the results of the survey, the Office estimated that there are approximately 551,000 female-operated and 1,313,000 male-female jointly operated enterprises in the MEL file. Female-operated businesses make up 9.5 percent of all businesses in the file. The MEL file itself is a mailing list which, according to SBA, "represents virtually all firms and establishments in the United States."[44] MEL is an invaluable new survey resource which can help improve the

---

[43]See for example, House Committee on Small Business, Women in Business: Hearings before the Subcommittee, on Minority Enterprise and General Oversight, 95th Congress, 1st session, April 5, May 24, June 1, 1977.

[44]U.S. Small Business Administration, State of Small Business, (1985), 415.

reliability of research conclusions by assuring that surveys can be administered to statistically valid samples.

The MEL file was used by the JACA Corporation to select a sample for an SBA-sponsored study to determine if there are differences in access to credit by men and women business owners.[45] The JACA study, which will be released in 1986, is the first of its kind. The study surveyed 400 male-operated and 400 female-operated businesses selected from the Small Business Data Base.

Another shortcoming of existing research on women's business ownership is the lack of a rigorous definition of a woman-owned business. As mentioned earlier, the SBA's Office of Women's Business Ownership utilizes the definition: "51 percent ownership, operation and control by a woman or women."[46] Most of the studies cited in this bibliography have not utilized a rigorous definition. To improve comparability among research findings, future studies should utilize the same definition of the woman-owned business.

Many of the studies cited in this bibliography fail to make use of control groups for comparison purposes. Survey samples are frequently made up entirely of women. In some of the cited studies, results are compared with the findings of earlier studies of male entrepreneurs, the female population as a whole, or women managers. Such comparisons are usually not advisable. The accepted procedure to yield the most reliable results involves testing against a control group drawn through the same sampling methods, at the same time, under the same conditions, and, in particular, using the same survey instrument(s).

Finally, because of their reliance on non-random samples of fewer than 30 women business owners, many studies such as those conducted by Schwartz, Schreier, Goffee, Seane, Nielsen, and Waddell are akin to case studies. Popular guides to business ownership for women often provide similar information of almost identical "scientific value" by presenting short profiles of successful women business owners.[47] If carried out in a systematic way, case studies can serve a valuable purpose by disclosing details and providing insights about the subject that go undetected by more scientifically implemented survey research. Case studies can also be very useful as pilots for research or as aids in designing questionnaires to be used for survey research. Nevertheless, findings from case studies or from surveys that employ very small samples cannot be generalized to the population as a whole, and are

---

[45]JACA Corporation (Faith Ando, principal investigator), "Access to Capital and/or Credit by Subcategories of Small Business," Office of Economic Research, U.S. Small Business Administration, publication expected 1986.

[46]See also Interagency Task Force, The Bottom Line, 11-12.

[47]See, for example, Charlotte Taylor, Women and the Business Game: Strategies for Successful Ownership (New York: Cornerstone Library, 1980); and Claudia Jessup and Genie Chipps, The Woman's Guide to Starting a Business (New York: Holt, Reinhart and Winston, 1980).

thus of little more value than the anecdotal information found in popular literature.

The small samples used in many of the studies of women entrepreneurs listed in this bibliography present a number of major problems for causal analysis. For example, it is often impossible to determine whether business problems women reported in these studies are related to gender, firm size, industry, type of business, geographic area in which a business was operated, to a combination of these, or to other factors.

Barriers to Entrepreneurship for Women

While it is not surprising that researchers have discovered many personal traits common to business owners of both sexes, women entrepreneurs, because they are women, experience different life patterns than do men, and may therefore have different experiences in starting and operating a business. Indeed, much of the existing literature takes great pains to point out the connections between the overall socioeconomic status of women and the status of the woman business owner. One observer stated the problem this way:

> Women are no different than men in their entrepreneurial drive and their desire for the economic independence and personal self-fulfillment that business ownership can bring. However, there is a catch. It tends to be more difficult for women than for men to live out this drive.[48]

Although the studies reviewed in preparing this bibliography often concluded that there were few measurable personal trait differences between men and women entrepreneurs, they also noted that the female population as a whole may face formidable barriers to successful business ownership, especially in particular industries.

Demarest, Hisrich and O'Brien, Finney and Schreier have all made a distinction between industry categories that are "traditional" and those that are "non-traditional" for women. Hisrich and O'Brien's work identifies business problems encountered by women by the type of business operated.[49] They found that female entrepreneurs in "non-traditional" business areas (finance, insurance, manufacturing and construction) often faced different issues then did women who owned more "traditional" businesses (in retail and wholesale trade, for example). Of particular importance was the apparent paucity of

---

[48]Taylor, Business Game, 16.

[49]In addition to the works by these authors mentioned above, see also, Robert Hisrich and Marie O'Brien, "The Woman Entrepreneur from a Business and Sociological Perspective," Proceedings, 1981 Conference on Entrepreneurship, (Boston: Babson College, 1981), 21-39.

external financing sources for women owners of "non-traditional" businesses.[50] The distinction Finney makes between "traditionally male" and "traditionally female" businesses is analogous to another distinction common in the literature on small business—between growth-oriented (type A) and limited growth (type B) businesses. Although the majority of women-owned businesses are probably "type B," Smith, McCain and Warren suggest that women entrepreneurs are more likely to exhibit "type A" personal characteristics than are men.[51] Despite this, it may still be true that the barriers to entrepreneurship women face are more substantial with respect to "type A" activities (i.e., growth-oriented ventures).

Although growth is probably difficult for all entrepreneurs to handle, the works of Hisrich and O'Brien, Bloom and Shaffer, and others suggest it may be a greater problem for women because of the particular social and economic barriers they must confront.[52] In contrast, Gregg argues in a recent article that a new generation of more successful and technically competent women entrepreneurs is emerging, and that this "second generation" may have less difficulty moving forward with growth-oriented ventures than did their predecessors.[53]

Most potential small business owners face certain obstacles, such as scarcity of adequate financial resources, formidable government regulation and taxation, and fluctuating economic conditions.[54] Research suggests that these common problems may be exacerbated by unique handicaps afflicting women more than men. These handicaps include lack of business training and experience; lack of financial skills; lack of access to capital; factors related to the type of business typically owned by women --low income and low equity, small size, low growth; management difficulties--factors such as management style,

---

[50]Lack of access to capital (including personal resources) is seen as a major reason for the concentration of women-owned businesses in service and retail. See, among others, Patricia McNamara, "Business Ownership: A New Career Option for Women," New Directions for Education, Work and Careers, (1979): 71-82.

[51]Smith, McCain, and Warren, "Women Entrepreneurs," 71.

[52]Hisrich and O'Brien, "Business and Sociological Perspective" and "Type of Business"; Bloom and Shaffer," Women-Owned Businesses: A Concept Paper" (Potomac, Md.: Paradigm, Inc., 1978, mimeographed); McNamara, "Business Ownership" Calvin Kent, "Entrepreneurship Education for Women: A Research Review and Agenda" (October 1982, available from the author, Hankhamer School of Business, Baylor University, Waco, TX).

[53]Gail Gregg, "Women Entrepreneurs: The Second Generation," Across the Board 22, 1 (January 1985), 10-18.

[54]For a concise discussion of these barriers, see Karl H. Vesper, Entrepreneurship and National Policy, (Chicago: Walter E. Heller International Corporation, Institute for Small Business, 1983).

inexperience or difficulties with financial management and planning; unique personnel management problems; the added burden of family responsibilities; and sex-role socialization-- which leads women to think small and cautiously, perpetuating the traditional helping role of women, the antithesis of risk-taking. While these problems/barriers are interrelated, we will discuss them here under four general headings --social; educational; economic and financial; and legal and institutional.

Social Barriers

Although most observers describe business ownership as a non-traditional career for women, the fact is that women have been involved in owning businesses for a very long time. Caroline Bird's book, Enterprising Women, documents the experience of American women entrepreneurs from the colonial period.[55] Until recently, however, women have played a hidden role in business as silent partners or unpaid workers in family businesses; or they have operated small enterprises out of their homes.

Experts on the family business point out that while a woman's direct and indirect contributions to the family business may have been of vital importance, she was usually not expected to take an open leadership role.[56] Sons (and sons-in-law), but not daughters, were groomed to take over the business. This pattern may be changing. One trainer in this field pointed out that recent enrollments for the family business succession courses offered by her firm have gone from 99 percent male to nearly half female.[57]

The explosion of computer technology and the advent of the "information age" have increased public awareness of new possibilities for home-based businesses. Futurists such as Toffler predict the computer will lead to a new era of cottage industry, with decentralized production by small, home-based operations linked to the market by terminals.[58] This trend toward decentralization is noted by Naisbitt.[59] Although women have been very actively involved in home-based businesses, little research has been done on their activities. The Census Bureau's report on Selected Characteristics of Women

[55]Caroline Bird, Enterprising Women (New York: Norton, 1976).

[56]Pat B. Alcorn, Success and Survival in the Family-Owned Business (New York: McGraw-Hill, 1982).

[57]Katy Danco, From the Other Side of the Bed: A Woman Looks at Life in the Family Business (Cleveland, OH.: Center for Family Business, 1981).

[58]Alvin Toffler, The Third Wave (New York: William Morrow, 1980).

[59]John Naisbitt, Megatrends: Ten New Directions Transforming Our Lives (New York: Warner Books, 1982). The author has also recently discovered the increasing importance of women in American social, political and economic life. See "The Eleventh Megatrend," Esquire, May 1983, 138.

<u>Owned Businesses</u> in 1977 found that 47 percent of the women business owners surveyed operated their businesses from their homes, while a more recent article emanating from research staff at the Internal Revenue Service suggests that 63 percent of female sole proprietors do business from home.[60] Yet most of the recent writings on home-based businesses are journalistic and advice oriented, offering little in the way of in-depth analysis.[61]

Over half of the respondents to the Hisrich and O'Brien survey of women business owners in Massachusetts cited as a significant problem "overcoming society's beliefs that women are not as serious as men about business."[62] In their responses to other surveys and interviews, women business owners often reported encountering active sex bias stemming from socialization (of themselves and others) and sex-related stereotyping. For the majority of women business owners surveyed, this was not identified as the most serious problem faced in operating their businesses, but it was invariably mentioned. This type of constraint has been thoroughly documented and explored in the literature on women in non-traditional occupations as well as in numerous studies on women managers.[63]

Both Finney and Demarest discovered that a sizeable proportion of the women business owners they interviewed were reluctant to think of their activities in terms of competition, preferring to stress the quality of their work and their ability to serve the needs of others through their businesses. Finney and Demarest argue that such an approach to business was more compatible with these women's image of femininity, which they had been socialized to value and preserve.[64]

---

[60]Bureau of the Census, <u>Selected Characteristics</u>, 16. See also Paul Grayson, <u>SOI Bulletin</u> (Spring 1983): 35.

[61]The following works from this genre stand out: Marion Behr and Wendy Lazar, <u>Women Working Home: The Home-Based Business Guide and Directory</u> (New Jersey: WWH Press, 1981); and Stuart Feldstein, <u>Home, Inc.: How to Start and Operate a Successful Business from Your Home</u> (New York: Grosset and Dunlap, 1981).

[62]Hisrich and O'Brien, "Business and Sociological Perspective," 27.

[63]For an overview of the earlier literature on women in non-traditional occupations, see KOBA Associates, Inc., <u>Women in Non-Traditional Occupations--A Bibliography</u> (Washington, D.C.: U.S. Department of Health, Education and Welfare, 1976). On women managers, see Rosabeth Kanter, <u>Men and Women of the Corporation</u> (New York: Basic Books, 1977); and Margaret Hennig and Anne Jardim, <u>The Managerial Woman</u> (Garden City, N.J.: Anchor Press/ Doubleday, 1977).

[64]Finney, <u>Towards a Typology</u>; Janice Demarest, "Women Minding Their Own Businesses: A Pilot Study of Independent Business and Professional Women and Their Enterprises" (Ph.D. diss., University of Colorado, 1977).

In his study of the educational needs of women business owners, Kent points out that women who might otherwise want to start their own ventures are inhibited by a lack of female role models.[65] Women may not receive the encouragement from family and peers they need to launch a business venture; and they may not have access to traditional business networks that provide contacts and assistance because these contacts are often found in clubs and associations restricted to men only.

On the other hand, some have argued that the same type of social bias that inhibits the movement and advancement of women in certain occupations and activities may stimulate them to start their own businesses. Divorced and widowed women, displaced homemakers, or women who have encountered obstacles in climbing the corporate ladder may try to succeed on their own by going into business for themselves.[66]

Studies of entrepreneurship (most notably the work of Shapero, Collins and Moore) have documented the influence that social factors such as displacement have in motivating individuals toward entrepreneurship.[67] They found that displacing events such as war, emigration, divorce or loss of employment can stimulate a person to start an independent business. Shapero argues that being "out of place" or "between jobs" is a common antecedent to new enterprise creation. Surprisingly little attention has been paid to the phenomenon of displacement as it might relate to women business owners. Nielsen's study of older women making a mid-life or mid-career move into business ownership only touched on the issue.[68] Many surveys of women business owners document marital status (while the majority have been married, many are divorced or widowed),[69] but the available evidence cannot confirm or deny claims that women business owners are "the new immigrants," moving into entrepreneurship as a result of some displacing event.[70]

Clearly, small business ownership does represent an employment alternative for women, just as it did for immigrants. Research on entrepreneurship has

---

[65]Kent, "Entrepreneurship Education," 8-10.

[66]Taylor, Women and the Business Game; and "Women Rise as Entrepreneurs," Business Week (Industrial Edition), February 25, 1980, 86-87.

[67]Shapero and Sokol, "Social Dimensions"; Orvis Collins and David Moore, The Organization Makers: A Behavioral Study of Independent Entrepreneurs (New York: Meredith, 1970).

[68]Lucille Nielsen, "An Exploratory-Descriptive Study of Mid-Life Women Who Have Created First-Time Independent Businesses," (unpublished dissertation, University of Oregon, 1981).

[69]Interagency Task Force, The Bottom Line, 34-35; Bureau of Census, Women-Owned Businesses 1977, 8, 20; Robert Hisrich and Candida Brush, "Women Entrepreneurs Survey," Boston College, 1982 (mimeographed).

[70]Taylor, Business Game.

demonstrated the extensive involvement of immigrant groups in new venture creation.[71] Part of the reason for immigrants' high representation in business owner ranks may be that these groups often lack qualifications on paper, and their access to traditional, or accepted education and training channels has been limited. In order to achieve greater mobility they create employment for themselves through business ownership. But it remains to be seen whether, like immigrants, women will continue their rapid rate of entry into independent business ownership should the rate and level of representation of women in corporate management ranks increase.

Barriers to Education and Training

It has been argued that women business owners encounter the same problems as do other small business owners, but, in addition, lack training in essential aspects of commercial enterprise, such as accounting, marketing and business law.[72] Women business owners have directly expressed their needs for business management assistance and training. In the 1977 survey undertaken by the President's Task Force on Women Business Owners, women respondents indicated that management was their biggest problem after finance.[73] A woman's lack of training or familiarity with the skills necessary to operate a business may be due to a lack of employment opportunities for women in related fields. Prevailing social attitudes and norms may have steered women away from seeking preparation in these areas. Management weakness, whether because of lack of experience or incompetence, is now believed to be the primary cause of small business failure regardless of the gender of the owner.[74] Therefore, technical and managerial experience and on-the-job business skill-building is crucial to the successful operation of a business.

Today, women are better educated than ever before, and more women are trained in business fields every year. But the progress women have made in employment has been much slower, and women who have penetrated the corporate management ranks are concentrated in less directly business-related areas such

---

[71]Shapero and Sokol, "Social Dimensions".

[72]Carol Eliason, Entrepreneurship for Women: An Unfulfilled Agenda (Columbus, OH: Ohio State University, National Center for Research on Vocational Education, 1981). Another recent (1982) treatment of necessary entrepreneurial competencies as identified by women service and retail business owners in Kansas can be found in Judy Diffley, "A Study of Women Business Owners and the Importance of Selected Entrepreneurial Competencies Related to Educational Programs" (Ph.D. diss., University of Oklahoma, 1982).

[73]Interagency Task Force, The Bottom Line, 49.

[74]Dun and Bradstreet Corp., Business Failure Record (New York: Dun and Bradstreet Corporation, Business Economics Division, 1980).

as personnel.[75] Nevertheless, recent surveys of women business owners show that those who are successful normally do have a good deal of employment experience in areas related to their current business and in management.[76] There is also evidence that in some industrial categories, their level of education may be higher than the population as a whole, and some studies comparing male and female entrepreneurs show that these women may be more educated than their male counterparts.[77]

It is often argued that entrepreneurs and managers are two very different types. But while arguments rage in the entrepreneurship studies field over whether managers can become successful entrepreneurs, some predict that many women will leave the ranks of corporate management for business ownership, should opportunities for women's advancement to executive levels continue to be limited.[78]

In the past 10 to 15 years, a large number of books and articles have appeared on the subject of women in corporate management.[79] These have focused on the problems women managers face because of sex stereotyping and the tendency for the organizational structures of corporations to reproduce male exclusivity in upper management. Attitudes toward women in management and their status in the corporate environment may be changing. Recent polls

---

[75]Mary Lou Randour, Georgia Strasburg and Jean Lipman-Blumen, "Women in Higher Education: Trends in Enrollments and Degrees Earned," Harvard Educational Review 52 (May 1982): 189-202.

[76]Hisrich and Brush, "Survey"; Interagency Task Force, The Bottom Line; Bureau of Census, Women-Owned Businesses, 1977, 30-31.

[77]This point is debatable. No firm conclusion can be drawn about the level of education of women entrepreneurs with respect to their male counterparts because studies which examine this question have relied on all-female samples or on samples too small to allow for firm conclusions. Welsch and Young, who compared women and men entrepreneurs directly, found the women were more educated. In addition, surveys by Diffley, the President's Task Force, The American Management Association and the Census Bureau all showed that women entrepreneurs are well-educated.

[78]"Women Rise as Entrepreneurs," Business Week, 86.

[79]A selected list of references on this topic appears in Appendix A of this document.

and surveys indicate that women are now being more readily accepted as managers and executives by their male colleagues and employees of both sexes.[80]

Researchers have agreed that women business owners lack science-related and technical education, as well as knowledge of practical finance-related skills necessary for business survival. As a result, new educational programs have been designed specifically for women business owners, and a number of papers have been written describing these programs and analyzing their results. One such effort was the U.S. Small Business Administration's pre-business workshops for women offered on an experimental basis through local SBA offices nationwide in 1977 and 1978.[81] The workshops were designed to provide participants with information on business organization, record keeping, financial resources, taxes, etc., so that they could make more informed decisions about whether to pursue business ownership.

A program developed in 1980-1981 by the National Association of Bank Women (NABW), sponsored by the Chemical Bank, and funded by the Donner Foundation and the U.S. Small Business Administration, was targeted at "successful" women business owners, helping them to understand the financial alternatives available for expansion through interaction with bankers in a workshop situation.[82] Programs for women business owners include the ongoing, well-publicized American Woman's Economic Development Corporation (AWED) in New York City[83]; the experimental California Women Entrepreneurs Project, which conducted training sessions and designed a set of learning modules for women business owners in the Los Angeles area in 1977,[84] but is now defunct; and the St. Paul, Minnesota-based Women's Economic Development

---

[80]A 1982 Business Week/Harris poll showed that 94 percent of male executives surveyed felt that, "contributions of women executives in the company are more positive than negative." ("How Executives See Women in Management," Business Week, June 28, 1982, 10.) This compares very favorably with an earlier survey by Eleanor Schwartz (i.e., it shows an improvement in attitudes toward women executives): Eleanor Schwartz, The Sex Barrier in Business (Atlanta: Georgia State University, 1971) See also, Alma S. Baron and L. Abrahamsen, "Will He--or Won't He--Work with a Female Manager?" Management Review (November 1981: 48-53).

[81]George Solomon, National Women's Pre-Business Workshop Evaluation Study (Washington, D.C.: U.S. Small Business Administration, 1979).

[82]Robert A. Bassi, "A Credit to Banking," NABW (National Association of Bank Women) Journal (July/August 1981).

[83]Arthur D. Little, Inc., The American Woman's Economic Development Corporation (Washington, D.C.: Economic Development Administration, U.S. Department of Commerce, 1980).

[84]Patricia McNamara and Barbara McCaslin, The Women Entrepreneurs Project: Final Report (Los Angeles: Univesity of California/Los Angeles, 1978).

Corporation (WEDCO), the most recent program developed to help women start and operate businesses. Founded in 1984 as a non-profit corporation under the joint auspices of the Hubert H. Humphrey Institute of Public Affairs, Chrysa- lis -- a Center for Women, and Mainstay, WEDCO reports[85] that in its first 15 months of operation 157 start-up and 239 ongoing businesses were assist- ed. Loan packaging help was provided during this period to 52 businesses, and 12 businesses received WEDCO loans in amounts ranging from $300 to $10,000. WEDCO publishes a newsletter and workbooks, conducts workshops and provides counseling. WEDCO is a participant in a joint project, begun in 1985 in cooperation with the Corporation for Enterprise Development in Washington, D.C., the Center for New Horizons in Chicago and the Kenilworth/- Parkside Council in Washington, D.C. aimed at self-employment for low-income women. WEDCO counterparts were in the process of replication in Flint, Michigan and Chicago, Illinois as this bibliography went to press.

These business assistance programs join a whole host of practical guides for women business owners that have appeared in the last 5 to 10 years.[86] Although the popular guides are generally absent any solid research base, many of them do include a wealth of anecdotal information on women business owners.

In the literature, attention has also been given to the need to make girls aware of entrepreneurship as a career option from an early age. Research in the fields of education and sex-role socialization indicates that young women are steered away from non-traditional fields very early. Studies show that most have already narrowed their possible career choices to female-dominated fields by the time they leave elementary school.[87] In his review of educational needs for fostering women's business ownership, Kent argues that the development of materials to increase the awareness of female school children about entrepreneurship as a career option, as well as efforts to reduce sex stereotyping in the schools, and the development of materials that emphasize the importance of women business owners to the economy, are crucial to the preparation of future women entrepreneurs.[88] Focusing on older students,

---

[85]WEDCO: Celebrating Two Years, (St. Paul, Minnesota: Women's Economic Development Corporation, Fall 1985), Newsletter. For further information, write to WEDCO, Iris Park Place Suite 395, 1885 University Avenue West, St. Paul, Minnesota, 55104.

[86]A list of selected recent contributions in this area is included in the "Education and Training for Women Entrepreneurs" section of the bibliography.

[87]Aimee Leifes and Gerald Lasser, The Development of Career Awareness in Children, National Institute of Education, Papers on Education and Work, (Washington, D.C.: U.S. Department of Health, Education and Welfare, National Institute of Education, 1976); also cited by the Interagency Task Force, The Bottom Line, 41.

[88]Kent, "Entrepreneurship Education," 14-15; See also, Carsrud et. al., "Some Observations", 14-15.

those returning to school after a long absence and non-credit students, the American Association of Community and Junior Colleges has designed a counseling model and curriculum package targeted at women who want to go into business for themselves.[89]

Economic/Financial Barriers

Extensive references are made throughout the literature on women business owners to support the connection between the economic status of women in the labor force and the status of women as business owners. Many authors agree with Hisrich and O'Brien that "the disadvantaged position of women in the economy is further reflected in the category of self-employed persons."[90] Indeed, earnings data show that self-employed women earn only 45 percent of what similarly situated men earn. Among wage and salary workers, women fare only slightly better--the annual earnings of year-round full-time women workers are 57 percent of corresponding earnings for men.[91] This differential is due, in large part, to the fact that women's employment is concentrated in a few occupations which are low-paying and offer little chance for advancement.[92] Bloom and Shaffer argue that occupational segregation persists despite the fact that federal laws prohibit sex discrimination in hiring, promotion and pay for four reasons. First, women traditionally have had inadequate access to certain types of employment opportunities. At the same time, most women have chosen not to pursue alternatives in non-traditional occupations. In addition, they have not always made use of legal protection and assistance available to them. And, finally, some employers' negative attitudes about women's skills and desire to work (which are based on old stereotypes, and, are generally unfounded) affect the access of women to many well-paying jobs.[93]

The rapid rate at which women are starting their own businesses suggests that women find entrepreneurship an increasingly important vehicle for economic

---

[89]Carol Eliason, Women Business Owners Orientation Program Guide (Washington, D.C.: AACJC, 1979).

[90]Hisrich and O'Brien, "Business and Sociological Perspective," 21

[91]Bureau of Labor Statistics, Monthly Income, table 58; see also Victor F. Fuchs, His and Hers: Gender Differences in Work and Income, 1959-1979 (Working Paper Number 1507), (Cambridge, MA: National Bureau of Economic Research, 1984)

[92]See, for example, Nancy S. Barrett, "Obstacles to Economic Parity for Women," The American Economic Review 72 (May 1982): 160-165; Janet L. Norwood, The Male-Female Earnings Issue, Report #673 (Washington, D.C.: U.S. Department of Labor, Bureau of Labor Statistics, September 1982); and Nancy F. Rytina, "Occupational Segregation and Earnings Differences by Sex," Monthly Labor Review (January 1981): 49-53.

[93]Bloom and Shaffer, "Women-Owned Businesses," 17.

viability. Although researchers seem to be unanimous that this is the case, they also point out that the disadvantages women face in the labor market may carry over into their business endeavors.[94] Just as women are concentrated in certain employment fields, so are women's businesses concentrated in certain industries.

Occupational segregation of women in the labor market affects potential women business owners in two ways. First, lack of employment opportunities for women in certain professions or occupations means that women entrepreneurs may find some important avenues to training and experience are blocked.

Second, occupational segregation and low income have a cumulative effect, limiting the access women have to credit and capital, and limiting their mobility among different sectors of the economy. Also, women's lower incomes affect their ability to accumulate equity in their businesses.[95] Savings from personal income and accumulated personal wealth are major sources of start-up funds for all small businesses, as are loans and equity investments from family and friends.[96] Many of the surveys of women small business owners have shown that they are no exception in relying heavily on personal savings and assets for initial capitalization of their ventures. The Bottom Line, for example, reported that 67 percent of women's start-up capital comes from their own resources or from friends and relatives.[97] A 1982 survey by Hisrich and Brush also found that personal assets and savings were by far the most important sources of initial financing.[98] Eighty-three percent of the

----

[94]In addition to Bloom and Shaffer and Hisrich and O'Brien, others who discuss this connection explicitly include: Schwartz (1976); McNamara (1979); President's Interagency Task Force on Women Business Owners; Callie Foster Struggs, Women in Business (Mesquita, TX: Ide House, 1981); and Jane Roberts Chapman, "Sex Discrimination in Credit: the Backlash of Economic Dependency," Economic Independence for Women, J.R. Chapman, ed. (Beverly Hills, CA.: Sage Publications, 1976).

[95]Interagency Task Force, The Bottom Line, 25-26; Bloom and Shaffer, "Women-Owned Businesses," 13; McNamara, "Business Ownership"; Hisrich and O'Brien, "Business and Sociological Perspective," 21.

[96]Research on business start-ups indicates that, on the average, from 80 to 100 percent of initial capital comes from family and friends. See Richard Morse, "The Capital Gap," Setting The Research Agenda: Proceedings of the Bentley Small Business Conference (Waltham, MA: Bentley College, 1981); Michael Keishnick, Venture Capital and Urban Development (Washington, D.C.: Council of State Planning Agencies, 1979); Albert Shapero, "Pre-Venture Capital: A Critical but Neglected Issue," The Entrepreneurial Economy 2 (July 1983): 3-4.

[97]Interagency Task Force, The Bottom Line, 60.

[98]Hisrich and Brush, "Women Entrepreneurs Survey."

respondents to the 1977 survey of women business owners said they obtained their start-up funds from family, friends and personal savings.[99]

In many of the studies reviewed, women business owners reported that their major business problem was not being able to obtain adequate financing for their operations. Indeed, this problem is often cited by all small business owners, male and female. Market imperfections associated with high information and transactions costs and the resulting capital rationing, and risk averse behavior by banks, make for difficulty in obtaining credit for all small businesses.[100] Because women-owned businesses are typically very small and concentrated in service and retail industries, banks and venture capital firms may find it even less attractive to invest in those types of businesses. Thus, women may suffer disproportionately from market imperfections which serve to limit overall small business access to private capital markets.

In a review of statistics on women business owners, Charlboneau argued that the greatest obstacle for women is dealing with the banking and financial community, which is overwhelmingly male.[101] Pilot programs have sought to overcome this barrier by conducting workshops for women owners, involving bankers as session leaders or participants. The National Association of Bank Women's workshops described earlier, were fielded hoping that close interaction would help to eliminate barriers to communication and misunderstandings between the two groups.[102]

The necessity of reliance on informal networks for start-up capital and initial loans may cause women to be at a distinct disadvantage because they are not as "well-connected" as men. Researchers point out that, historically, women have been discriminated against in the business world; they have encountered barriers to entering and advancing in certain kinds of jobs such as management and banking. In addition, women are often barred from admission to business clubs and associations where many contacts are made[103]— contacts that may prove essential for arranging informal financing. Although efforts have recently been made to investigate the nature and importance of

---

[99]Bureau of the Census, Women-Owned Businesses, 1977.

[100]See Morse, "Capital Gap," Keishnick, Venture Capital, and Shapero, "Pre-Venture Capital." See also Lawrence Litvake and Belden Daniels, Innovations in Development Finance (Washington, D.C.: Council of State Planning Agencies, 1979).

[101]Jill F. Charlboneau, "The Woman Entrepreneur," American Demographics (June 1981): 21-23.

[102]Robert Bassi, "A Credit to Banking," NABW (National Association of Bank Women) Journal (July/August, 1981).

[103]Lynn Hecht Schafran, "Welcome to tne Club! (No Women Need Apply)" Women and Foundations/Corporate Philanthropy (February 1982).

informal risk-capital networks for small business no attempt has yet been made to distinguish between the experiences of men and women-owned businesses in these studies.[104]

The literature that deals with women's access to credit (both consumer and commercial credit) identifies two barriers to credit access for women: low earnings and net personal worth, and discrimination. In the 1970's, the belief that women were being discriminated against in the allocation of credit contributed to the formation of women's banks, as well as to passage of the Equal Credit Opportunity Act (ECOA) of 1974.

Aside from a few brief references to women-owned businesses in papers on small business finance and a couple of articles on the application of ECOA to commercial lending,[106] nearly all that has been written on women and credit focuses exclusively on consumer credit. Even evidence of discrimination in commercial and consumer credit used to justify ECOA was largely anecdotal. One statistically-based study, conducted using pre-ECOA data, purports to show that commercial banks were not discriminating against women in consumer credit at the time the ECOA was passed.[106]. Similarly, studies of the mortgage market by Massachusetts Institute of Technology economists Ladd and Schaffer showed almost no incidence of sex bias in mortgage lending, although attempts at revision of Federal Housing Administration regulations had been undertaken to prevent sex discrimination in mortgage lending.[107]

---

[104]Albert Shapero, "Role of Financial Institutions of a Community in the Foundation, Effectiveness, and Expansion of Innovating Companies" (Columbus, OH: Shapero-Huffman Associates, 1983), SBA contract #2654-OA-79; William Wetzel, "Informal Risk Capital in New England" (Durham, NH: University of New Hampshire, 1980); William Wetzel, "Risk Capital Research," in Encyclopedia of Entrepreneurship, ed. Kent, Sexton, and Vesper, 133.

[105]See Chapman. "Sex Discrimination"; William Dearhammer, "Equal Credit Opportunity Act/Regulation B--Application to Business Credit," Journal of Commercial Bank Lending 61 (January 1979): 20-36.

[106]Richard L. Peterson, "An Investigation of Sex Discrimination in Commercial Bank Lending," Bell Journal of Economics 12 (Autumn 1981): 547-561.

[107]Robert Schaffer and Helen Ladd, Equal Credit Opportunity: Accessibility to Mortgage Funds by Women and by Minorities: Final Technical Report (Washington, D.C.: U.S. Government Printing Office, 1980).

Studies of consumer credit repayment suggest that, on the whole, women may be a better credit risk than men.[108] But the only information now available on commercial credit by gender of business owner/borrower is provided by Glassman and Struck, who examined charge-off rates for commercial bank loans. They found that charge-off rates were equal or slightly lower for loans to women-owned businesses, supporting other reports that women are at least as good credit risks as are men.[109]

In 1983, the U.S. Small Business Administration awarded a contract for research on access to business credit and capital by sub-categories (minority and women) of small business owners.[110] The study, which is expected to be released in early 1986, utilizes a stratified random sample of 400 male and 400 female small business owners drawn from SBA's new small business data base. This will be the first major supply-side study of commercial credit and business capital access by gender of business owner. Results were not yet reportable as this bibliography went to press.

Legal Barriers[111]

The most basic workings of business presuppose a conducive legal environment. For women business owners, as for all business owners, the legal environment must permit the entrepreneur to own and purchase goods and services, to obtain credit and financing, to have access to affordable insurance coverage, and to remain solvent after government taxation.

Over the years, several research studies and analyses have focused on women's legal rights, but few have examined directly the legal barriers faced by

---

[108]P.F. Smith, "Measuring Risk on Installment Credit," Management Science 2 (November 1964): 327-340; R.F. Kerr, "Statement" in Hearings Before the Subcommittee on Consumer Affairs, Committee on Banking and Currency, on H.R. 14856 and H.R. 14908, June 21, 1974 (Washington, D.C.: U.S. Government Printing Office, 1974). Both of the above are cited in Chapman, "Sex Discrimination," 270-271.

[109] Cynthia Glassman and Peter Struck, "Survey of Commercial Bank Lending to Small Business," Studies of Small Business Finance (Washington, D.C.: The Interagency Task Force on Small Business Finance, 1982), 72-73, 80, 82.

[110]Faith Ando, Access to Capital and/or Credit by Subcategories of Small Business (Fort Washington, PA: JACA Corp.) Publication expected 1986. SBA contract #6061-0A-82.

[111]This section was prepared by legal consultant Robin Murez. See part two of this bibliography for a more detailed treatment of these issues.

women entrepreneurs.[112] The research available on women business owners does suggest that women's legal rights to engage in business in the United States continue to be somewhat restricted. For example, vestiges of European legal tradition in a few states continue to restrict the degree of control and ownership of a business a woman may retain when she marries.[113]

Also, although state and federal legislation aimed at prohibiting sex discrimination in lending to non-business credit applicants has been enacted (i.e., Truth in Lending, Fair Credit Billing, Fair Credit Reporting, and Consumer Leasing Acts), questions have arisen as to whether the Equal Credit Opportunity Act's protections extend to business loans as well as to consumer credit. A Federal Reserve Board rulemaking was proposed in 1978 to apply the ECOA protections to business credit.[114] In October 1982, the Board withdrew the proposed rulemaking after receiving numerous opposing comments from banks; and fewer supporting comments from public interest groups, women's rights organizations and government civil rights offices. The Board found that the inconvenience to banks posed by the mechanical requirements of the rulemaking outweighed the benefits to business applicants.

Another area affecting the legal rights of women business owners which has been debated in Congress and throughout the insurance industry is the availability of fair and affordable insurance coverage.[115] Because a majority of women business owners are sole proprietors, individual insurance policies for life, health, disability, property and casualty insurance are also critical to the survival of the sole proprietorship. Life insurance policy premiums have been generally higher for women than for men because of gender-based actuarial tables. Since these policies are frequently required as collateral for business loans the result is a higher cost of doing business for women

---

[112]   Shana Alexander and Barbara Brudno, State by State Guide to Women's Legal Rights (Los Angeles: Wollstonecraft, Inc., 1975); see also Interagency Task Force, The Bottom Line, 149-152. Barbara Babcock, Ann Freedman, Eleanor Holmes Norton and Susan Ross, Sex Discrimination and the Law, Causes and Remedies, (Little, Brown and Co., Boston: 1975) supplement by Wendy Williams, 1978. Davidson, Ginsburg and Herna Hill Kay, Text, Cases and Materials on Sex-Based Discrimination, 2nd edition, (West Publishing Co., MN: 1974), supplemented by Kay and Ginsburg, 1981, supplemented by Kay, 1983.

[113]Karen DeCrow, Sexist Justice (New York: Random House, 1974). Philip Francis, Legal Status of Women (Dobbs Ferry, New York: Oceana Publications, 1978).

[114]43 Federal Register 203 (October 26, 1978) Reg B Docket No. R-0185

[115]House Committee on Energy and Commerce, Nondiscrimination in Insurance Act of 1981: Hearing before the Subcommittee on Transportation and Tourism, 97th Congress, 1st Session, May 20, 1981 (Serial 97-22). See H.R. 100 and S. 2477 caselaw following City of Los Angeles Department of Water and Power v. Manhart, 435 U.S. 702, 55 L Ed 2nd 98 Section 1370 (1978).

than for men.[116] Historically, Congress has left regulation of the insurance industry in the hands of state legislators; but, with growing public criticism and lawsuits implicating insurance practices, the U.S. Congress has been increasingly active in considering public policy which will prohibit sex discrimination in insurance.

Since most women business owners are sole proprietors, federal taxes are assessed according to their individual incomes. Legal analysts have generally found the U.S. Tax Code to be free of any gender bias which might cause a disparity in treatment between female and male tax-paying entrepreneurs. However, Roff takes issue with the use of gender-based life expectancy tables in the Internal Revenue Code.[117] Other researchers question the Tax Code's presumption that ownership and control of community property rests with the husband.[118]

Valuable business associations and informal "networks" are frequently developed by men through their participation in private clubs. Women are often barred from membership and participation in such clubs and thereby prevented access to important business networks. Legal analysts are presently examining the tax advantages available to male members of these private clubs, as a basis for challenging the discriminatory exclusion of women.[119] It is argued that, since schools receiving federal funding and tax advantages must comply with civil rights laws and Constitutional guarantees, so the potentially sex-discriminatory membership practices of these tax advantaged clubs should be carefully scrutinized.

A final legal concern which has drawn attention regards the technical, gender-specific grammatical inequities in the laws of the United States. A report by the United States Commission on Civil Rights highlighted the incidence of gender-specific terminology in the Federal Code; and States have supplied some state-level findings to the White House 50 States Project.[120] In August 1983, President Reagan authorized the removal of gender-specific terminology from the United States Code.

---

[116]Naomi Naierman, Ruth Brannon and Beverly Wahl, Sex Discrimination in Insurance: A Guide for Women (Washington D.C.: Women's Equity Action League, 1980). U.S. Commission on Civil Rights, Discrimination Against Minorities and Women in Pensions and Life and Disability Insurance, 2 vols. (Washington D.C.: U.S. Government Printing Office, 1978) vol. 1 proceedings and papers; vol. 2 documents. No. 005-000-00186-2.

[117]Douglas E. Roff, "Gender Based Mortality Tables and the Code: An Equal Protection Analysis," University of Florida Law Review 33 (1980): 122.

[118]Interagency Task Force, The Bottom Line.

[119]See The American Bar Association Journal (August 1982): 884, 1024.

[120]U.S. Commission on Civil Rights, Sex Bias in the United States Code (Washington D.C.: 1977), 221; U.S. Department of Commerce, White House Task Force, The 50 States Project: Status of Women (Washington D.C.: Executive Office of the President, Unpublished).

Government Assistance for Women Business Owners

The Federal Government has generated the majority of existing literature on women business owners. Over the past 10 years, government documentation of the barriers to women's business ownership has increased. Federal agencies have taken steps to address these barriers and assist women business owners in entering the U.S. economic mainstream, largely through attempts to make existing government efforts on behalf of all small business responsive to their needs. In addition, some government programs have been specifically designed to promote business ownership for women and to assist women already involved in business.[121] Documentation and evaluation of these initiatives abound in federal government publications and the Congressional Record.

Although the goal of economic independence for women has made women's business ownership a natural interest of the women's movement of the 1970's and 1980's, education, political rights and representation, reproductive rights, employment opportunities, and remuneration and other job-related issues have been and continue to be the movement's principal concerns. The Report of the National Commission on the Observance of International Women's Year (IWY Commission), ...To Form a More Perfect Union, focused briefly on obstacles to business ownership for women, including limited credit access, women's position in the labor force, and the family responsibilities of women.[122] A 1975 report by the U.S. Commission on Civil Rights, Minorities and Women as Government Contractors, concluded that women experience obstacles to conducting business that are similar, if not identical, to those faced by minorities.[123] Following similar reasoning, the IWY Commission recommended in its report that the President introduce an amendment to Executive Order 11625 to add women to its coverage and to the programs administered by the Office of Minority Business Enterprise at the U.S. Department of Commerce.[124]

In November, 1977, the first federal government-sponsored National Women's Conference was held in Houston, Texas as part of the U.S. Observance of the United Nations Decade for Women. The conference report recommended changes

---

[121]U.S. Interagency Committee on Women's Business Enterprise, Annual Report to the President (Washington, D.C.: U.S. Small Business Administration, 1980).

[122]U.S. Department of Labor, National Commission on the Observance of International Women's Year, "...To Form a More Perfect Union..." Justice for American Women (Washington, D.C.: U.S. Government Printing Office, 1977).

[123]U.S. Commission on Civil Rights, Minorities and Women as Government Contractors (Washington, D.C.: U.S. Civil Rights Commission, 1975).

[124]National Commission on International Women's Year, "...To Form a More Perfect Union...", 64.

in government policy to provide greater opportunities for U.S. women in general. Women's business ownership was identified in the report as an important area of concern. The report recommended that women business owners be included in the U.S. Small Business Administration's subcontracting set-aside program for socially and economically disadvantaged business owners (commonly known as the "8-a" program because its authorization is included in section 8(a) of the Small Business Act).[125]

The event that focused national attention on the problems of women business owners was the Congressional hearings held in the Spring of 1977. The hearings followed the publication, in late 1976, of the first census of women-owned businesses. The census had reported that women-owned businesses were only 4.6 percent of all U.S. firms and that they accounted for a tiny 0.3 percent of these firms' total gross receipts.[126] Policy-makers were eager to discover the causes of the weak economic position of women-owned businesses and to determine ways to improve it. The testimony of women business owners and their representatives revealed that many women who had successfully overcome economic, social and cultural barriers to become independent business owners felt they still faced discrimination and other barriers to business success.[127] These hearings and subsequent government-sponsored reports produced valuable insights into the problems and issues faced by women business owners, and focused attention on the need for additional research.

In 1977, following the Congressional hearings, the President created the Interagency Task Force on Women Business Owners, composed of high level representatives from seven federal departments and agencies.[128] The 1978 report produced by the Task Force, The Bottom Line: Unequal Enterprise in America, is still the most extensive work on women's business ownership in the United States. It draws on a review of the relevant literature available at the time, analyzes the results of a survey of 3,000 women business owners, closely examines the problems faced by women business owners, and makes detailed proposals for helping women overcome barriers to successful business ownership.

---

[125]U.S. Department of Labor, National Commission on the Observance of International Women's Year, The Spirit of Houston (Washington, D.C.: U.S. Government Printing Office, 1978).

[126]Bureau of the Census, Women-Owned Businesses, 1972, 1.

[127]House Committee on Small Business, Women in Business: Hearings before the Subcommittee on Minority Enterprise and General Oversight, 95th Congress, 1st session, April 5, May 24 and June 7, 1977; Senate Select Committee on Small Business, Women and the Small Business Administration, 94th Congress, 2nd session, February 24, 1976.

[128]Interagency Task Force, The Bottom Line, 3-4.

One month after the release of The Bottom Line, the President created an Interagency Committee on Women's Business Enterprise and charged it with finding ways of implementing the Task Force's recommendations. The Committee's most recent Annual Report was issued in 1980.[129]

Although earlier recommendations had sought to include women-owned firms as a category of minority and disadvantaged businesses under existing federal authorities, and specifically to make Executive Order 11625 on Minority Business Enterprise apply to them, it was eventually decided that women entrepreneurs could best be assisted with programs specifically for women. In May of 1979 a separate Executive Order (12138) was signed, creating a national policy on women's business enterprise.[130]

Since that time, the focus of government activity on behalf of women business owners has largely been centered in the Small Business Administration, where the Office of Women's Business Ownership (formerly Office of Women's Business Enterprise) has been located since the spring of 1980. Several other agencies and departments have also made substantial efforts to assist women in starting and expanding their own ventures. But the SBA has been the major source of technical assistance and management training programs for small business as well as a major commercial lender to small business, providing direct loans and loan guarantees. Thus, it was deemed appropriate that assistance programs for women business owners be centered at SBA.

The SBA has had special outreach and management assistance efforts for women business owners since 1977 when it launched a Women's Business Ownership Campaign.[131] Also in 1977, a series of 400 one-day pre-business workshops for women were held across the country attended by over 30,000 women. An SBA evaluation of the workshops concluded they were highly successful.[132] SBA also sponsored two-day regional seminars in the first half of 1978 for female entrepreneurs already in business. The Small Business Administration also serves many women in its regularly scheduled training activities. Several university-based Small Business Development Centers have undertaken special assistance and research programs related to women during this period--the Universities of Pennsylvania, Wisconsin and Georgia are noteworthy

---

[129]Interagency Committee, Annual Report; See also, "All the President's Women: Update on Progress of Interagency Committee on Women's Business Enterprise," Enterprising Women 1 (1979): 67.

[130]A copy of the Executive Order is included in the Appendix to this document. See also, "Federal Nurturing for Female Entrepreneurs," Nation's Business 67, 8 (August 1979): 77-78.

[131]"Business Women Get a Champion at SBA," Nations's Business 65, 12 (December 1977): 34-36.

[132]See Solomon, Evaluation Study.

examples.[133] In 1983, an SBA program piloted initially by the Office of Women's Business Ownership was fielded through all SBA District offices nationwide to conduct in-depth "survival" programs emphasizing financial management skills for women-owned businesses in the critical first three years of existence. Leader's guides, participant workbooks and instructional videotapes are available.[134]

In 1983-84, The National Initiative for Women's Business Ownership was spearheaded from SBA's Office of Women's Business Ownership which featured training conferences in 23 cities attended by nearly 30,000 present and potential women business owners, and the establishment of a blue-ribbon Presidential Advisory Committee on Women's Business Ownership. An evaluation of the conferences[135] is scheduled for release as this bibliography goes to press, as is the report of the Presidential Advisory Committee.[136]

Because of its size and the variety of products and services it buys, the Federal Government has the ability to aid in achieving national socioeconomic goals while fulfilling its supply needs. Access to government procurement for small, minority, and women-owned businesses has received a great deal of attention in Congressional hearings and press coverage of small business issues. The reports of the Task Force on Women Business Owners, the 1980 White House Conference on Small Business, and other documents have included many recommendations on federal access to procurement by present and potential women contractors.[137]

----

[133]Some of these projects/research are documented: Constance Williams, The Women's Project (Philadelphia: Small Business Development Center, The University of Pennsylvania, 1982); William Strang and James McConnell, The 1980 Wisconsin Beauty/Barber Shop Survey (Madison: University of Wisconsin, Small Business Development Center, 1981). The latter is one of the few studies in small business research that identifies the gender of the business owner.

[134]Office of Women's Business Ownership, Surviving Business Crises (Washington, D.C.: U.S. Small Business Administration, 1983). Available for review at District and Regional offices of the U.S. Small Business Administration in all states and Puerto Rico.

[135]Computer Systems Service Bureau, Inc., "Evaluation of the Women's Business Ownership Conferences '84" (Washington, D.C." U.S. Small Business Administration, Office of Women's Business Ownership, 1985.)

[136]Executive Office of the President, 1985

[137]Commission on International Women's Year, Houston; Interagency Task Force, The Bottom Line, 77-84; White House Conference on Small Business, America's Small Business Economy: Agenda for Action (Washington, D.C.: U.S. Government Printing Office, 1980).

The first documentation of issues of women and federal contracting is contained in a 1975 report by the U.S. Commission on Civil Rights which found women's participation in federal procurement to be less than that of minorities, and recommended that women business owners be included in the SBA's 8(a) subcontracting program for economically and socially disadvantaged business owners.[138] When the Civil Rights Commission report was updated in 1977, the Commission found that women-owned businesses continued to receive an insignificant portion of federal contracts; and again in 1983, research sponsored by the U.S. Small Business Administration's Office of Economic Research documented the very small proportion of contracts and subcontracts awarded to women's firms.[139]

The SBA's efforts to assist women in doing business with the Federal Government have included annual negotiation of agency procurement goals, a campaign to register more women for the Procurement Automated Source System (PASS), and efforts to increase women's awareness of this service. In addition, the SBA has funded research on successful and unsuccessful women bidders for federal contracts and their companies. The purpose of that study was to gather more information about the factors contributing to successful federal contracting in order to inform other women business owners interested in seeking federal contracts on the activities and approaches that produce the best results.[140]

The SBA sponsored a pilot mini-loan program in Fiscal Year 1980, providing loans for under $20,000 to women-owned businesses. Although the program was not continued, the satisfaction of the borrowers under the program has been reviewed in internal reports. Generally speaking, "mini-loan" recipients were happy with their experience, and SBA has documented that there is no sex-based difference in the pay-back history on SBA loans of this size to men and women.[141]. The SBA makes other loans and loan guarantees available to women-owned businesses on the same basis as other businesses. SBA lending patterns by sex were monitored and documented from 1979-1981. The Small Business Investment Corporations (SBIC's) and Minority Enterprise Small Business Investment Companies (MESBIC's) that receive matching funds from SBA and provide venture capital to small businesses have had very limited experience with lending to women-owned businesses. The Bottom Line reported that in

---

[138]Commission on Civil Rights, Minorities and Women.

[139]Ann P. Maust and Mary Greiner, "An Analysis of Smaller Firm Participation" (Washington, D.C.: U.S. Small Business Administration, November 1983.)

[140] Alice Gordon, Emily Lusker, and Meredith Webb, Women-Owned Small Businesses: Winning in the Federal Marketplace, 3 vols. (Washington, D.C.: CRC Education and Human Development, December 1981).

[141]Unpublished internal evaluations of the mini-loan program are available from the U.S. Small Business Administration, Office of Women's Business Ownership.

1977 one SBIC was formed with the expressed purpose of paying particular attention to women-owned businesses, but the project did not materialize.[142]

In recent years, the SBA has also sponsored research on women-owned businesses, and is now in the process of constructing a data base for research purposes, based on Dun and Bradstreet files.[143] A major SBA-sponsored evaluation of the ability of existing SBA programs to meet the needs of women business owners was funded, but never completed.[144] Another study of credit and capital access for women-owned firms sponsored by the SBA's Office of Economic Research is expected to be released in early 1986.

Conclusions: Future Research Needs

Women's business ownership remains largely neglected as a field for scholarly research. Most studies to date are small-scale, preliminary efforts. Many important questions have been left unanswered. More often, they have been barely mentioned.

Themes explored in existing research on women business owners center on social, cultural and psychological determinants of entrepreneurship and the personal characteristics of the entrepreneur.[145] Some few studies and reports have examined the impact of government programs and policies on women business owners, and have recommended various changes. Nevertheless, the treatment has been rather general, and has concentrated on very broad questions: Who is the woman business owner? How does she differ from her male counterpart? What, if any, may be her special needs? Although these questions are important ones, answers have been elusive, when answers have been attempted at all.

Research gaps are particularly evident with respect to the economic questions: access to credit and capital, comparison of profitability of male

---

[142]Interagency Task Force, The Bottom Line, 102.

[143]Small Business Administration, State of Small Business, 1985, 271-297, 320.

[144]The evaluation study was initiated at the request of the U.S. General Accounting Office; see U.S. General Accounting Office, Report to the Administrator, Small Business Administration: Need to Determine Whether Existing Programs Can Meet the Needs of Women Entrepreneurs (Washington, D.C.: U.S. General Accounting Office, 1981).

[145]See Robert D. Hisrich and Donald D. Bowen, "The Female Entrepreneur: A Career Development Perspective" Academy of Management Review (April 1986) for a useful summary of the research gaps in this area.

versus female-owned firms and determinants of the causes of any differentials found, the potential for growth, and the employment impact of female-owned firms.

Particularly striking is the absence of inquiry into the nature of the businesses women own, rather than the personality traits of the owners. All available data document that women are starting their own businesses at a rate much greater than the corresponding rate for men. Thus, barriers to entering business ownership that women face, although they may be different, are probably not much greater than those that men confront. Nevertheless, the relatively small size of women's businesses, and the persistence of low receipts pose questions that have not yet been adequately addressed. A serious and in-depth study of the relationship between the industrial distribution of firms by gender of owner and the differential economic status of men and women-owned firms would be particularly useful.

Research on women business owners and their firms has suffered greatly from the lack of appropriate and timely availability of data. One of the most obvious weaknesses in many of the studies cited in this bibliography is reliance on poorly drawn, unscientific samples and out-of-date information, including data which are often more than five years old. There seems to be little hope of remedying this situation--it is a problem that is relatively common to all small business research. The data provided by the once-every-five-years census of women-owned businesses can be supplemented with information on sole proprietorships from the Internal Revenue Service and the self-employment data from the Bureau of Labor Statistics. This is now being done to a certain degree in the annual reports on the state of small business, published by SBA. But the problem of maintaining a relatively complete, comparable, reliable source of data still remains. The SBA's data base developed from Dun and Bradstreet files may improve data gathering. It will at least provide a more consistent source of sampling for survey research, although repeated surveys of the business owners included in the data base could be a burden on the individuals involved and, if utilized too frequently, could result in decreasing response rates.

Another crucial research need is to incorporate, wherever feasible, the gender of the business owner as a category of analysis in relevant small business research. For example, a study of micro-businesses could yield a wealth of information on women-owned firms if gender of owner were included as a variable in the study. All available evidence points to the likelihood that the vast majority of women-owned businesses are very small. In fact, the 1977 Census stated that only 23.9 percent of women-owned firms were employer firms.[146] However, at the present time very little research is available on these micro-businesses. Any information generated on these enterprises would be of particular interest to policy makers.

It may not always be practical or desirable to investigate a particular question with respect to the gender of the business owner. This may be a

---

[146]Bureau of Census, Women-Owned Businesses, 1977, 8.

40

principal reason why, in both entrepreneurship and small business research the gender of the business owner/entrepreneur has rarely been considered. If such a variable were to be introduced in future survey research it would be important for appropriate sampling techniques to be used to ensure a reliable outcome from statistical tests.

In the near term, more serious consideration of women's business enterprise as a separate research topic, or as one among many issues to be examined within the field of entrepreneurship and small business studies, would certainly serve to enhance the existing body of knowledge on the subject, even if only incrementally. Looking to the future, the phenomenon of women's business ownership as a critical element in the emergence of a new national economy is certain to become more obvious. This will necessitate more timely and in-depth information to assure that the phenomenon is monitored for its economic impact; and so that policy and program initiatives are created that will enhance the ability of women's businesses to make the maximum possible contribution to the ongoing vitality of the U.S. economy.

Section II:
Legal Status of Women Business Owners
Overview

Women business owners, like all business owners, are vitally concerned with the sources, and terms and conditions of availability of the financial base so critical to the survival of a business enterprise.

In basic terms, funds are required at the outset of a business enterprise to purchase supplies, a work space, or to hire and coordinate assistance. As the business flourishes, attention must be given to the flow of funds through the business--to business expenditures and receipts--and safeguards must be developed against unforeseen irregularities in these basic mechanics.

These fundamental processes of business presuppose certain legal rights and privileges of the entrepreneur. The business owner must be legally permitted to engage in business, and to own and sell products or services. He or she must be legally capable of borrowing needed start-up monies and the privilege of receiving loan credit must be unmitigated. Further, the continued viability of the business enterprise depends upon the owner's right to receive appropriate insurance protections. Lastly, the financial base of every business in the United States is premised upon remaining solvent despite (or with the assistance of) government taxation.

Research and analysis cited in this bibliography reveal issues within this legal framework of special importance to women entrepreneurs. Briefly stated, these are:

The threshold question of whether women have the legal right to engage in business in the United States must be examined within the context of property rights. Legal analysis reveals that:

- in a few states legal "technicalities" require female, but not male, business owners to petition the state for the right to engage in business; and

- in a greater number of states, vestiges of our European legal traditions act as obstacles to the rights of married women to purchase, control and sell business property.

In recent years the problems surrounding women's access to credit have received the attention of lawmakers. A major piece of legislation, the Equal Credit Opportunity Act (ECOA), was enacted to protect the rights of women to receive fair treatment from lending institutions. However, analysis of ECOA and its regulations indicates that by application:

- its protections extend to consumer credit, but fall short of full protection of commercial credit transactions; and

- its regulations also provide exemptions to credit transactions involving community property. Some legal analysts voice concern that, in effect, women, and not men, applying for credit are detrimentally affected by this community property exemption.

State and federal legislatures and the courts have recognized the need to review insurance industry practices which directly and indirectly affect the availability, terms and rates of insurance:

- individual life insurance policies, (frequently required as collateral for loans to small business owners) are criticized for their dependence upon gender-based actuarial tables and the resulting high rates women are assessed;

- analysts also find that women face disparate treatment in health, disability, property and casualty insurance. (See also Social Security Tax Laws.)

Since most women in small business are sole proprietors, their federal taxes are based upon their individual income and expenditures. For the most part, legal analysts find that women entrepreneurs receive the same tax treatment as do similarly situated men. However, criticism has been raised regarding:

- the constitutionality of gender-based life expectancy tables (similar to those used in the insurance industry) used in the Internal Revenue Code in determining certain individual tax rates;

- a presumption in the Code that the ownership and control of community property automatically rest with the husband unless rebutted;

- the "benefits" (or rather, shortcomings) of social security tax laws as applied to women in business; and,

- a tax-related issue of the unregulated, discriminatory practices of private clubs (whose members receive business tax deductions) in barring women from membership and participation.

The legal issues of importance to women business owners in property rights, credit, insurance and taxation are summarized in this chapter. The bibliographic citations highlight the most pertinent recent publications on each topic. Analysis of general business concerns, or of women's rights in general, are only included wherein legal issues of specific importance to women business owners are reviewed.

Legal research focusing on issues of importance to women business owners is extremely limited. In an effort to identify the salient legal issues and to provide a bibliographic starting point for future research, the listing herein is enlarged beyond purely scholarly legal research. Additionally, an effort is made to provide topical summaries and annotations of the legal issues which do not necessitate extensive prior familiarity with the law, or with legal bibliographic form.

The publications cited include: scholarly analysis recently published in law journals, government-generated publications including legislative hearings and clearinghouse reports, instructional texts, and several practical guides to legal issues for the non-lawyer. Several valuable primary sources of ongoing analysis such as state commissions on the status of women and state insurance regulatory authorities are identified in the topical summaries.

The materials were collected through extensive computer and manual searches, and through consultations with experts in the public and private sectors. The computer search utilized Scorpio and Mums (the Library of Congress book and periodical retrieval systems) and Dialog (the Legal Resource Index program). Manual searches of the Legal Resource Index and the Index to Legal Periodicals, as well as the card catalogs of the Library of Congress, the Small Business Administration, the Department of Justice, the Commission on Civil Rights and the Georgetown University Law Center were conducted.

Consultations with experts in government included individuals at the Commission on Civil Rights, Federal Reserve Board, Department of Justice, Department of Labor, White House Task Force and Congressional Committees on Commerce, Finance and the Judiciary. Foundations and organizations lending information included the Business and Professional Women's Foundation, League of Women Voters, National Association of Women Business Owners, National Conference on State Legislatures, National Center on Women and Family Law, Urban Law Institute, Women's Equity Action League, and the Women's Legal Defense Fund.

Tax

Small businesses are subject to state and federal taxation as one of three business forms:

- Sole Proprietorships - The simplest form of business wherein an individual engages in business. Tax liability is assessed directly to the sole proprietor. This is the dominant form of women-owned small businesses.

- Partnerships - Two or more persons engaging in business jointly, sharing both profits and losses, are individually assessed taxes based on their percentage of ownership of the partnership. Partnerships include joint ventures, groups, pools, syndicates, and family owned businesses.

- Corporations - A business licensed under state laws as a corporation is assessed tax liability separate and apart from its joint stockholders/owners. Corporate profits are assessed directly to the corporation and, when distributed to shareholders/owners as dividends, to the shareholders. Corporate taxation is computed at different rates than sole proprietorships or partnerships. Few women-owned businesses are corporations.

As a result of recent amendments to the Tax Code, the tax treatment of women-owned small businesses (sole proprietorships, partnerships and corporations) does not differ greatly from the treatment of small businesses in general. However, three issues have been raised which reflect on the tax liability of the dominant form of women owned businesses, sole proprietorships.

- In a recent law review article, Roff challenges the constitutional validity of the Internal Revenue Code's use of gender-based mortality tables. The tables are used in the IRC to compute tax liability associated with annuity investments (including life insurance), and charitable trusts. Generally, women are assessed more burdensome taxes solely by virtue of their sex. Women in business are likely to put income and profits toward these sorts of investments and trusts (as discussed in the insurance section); therefore, as sole proprietors, women business owners are subject to more burdensome tax consequences than are similarly situated men owners.

- The second issue of importance to women business owners regards the underlying assumption in the Internal Revenue Code that income and deductions derived from a business (not including a partnership) in a community property state rest solely with the husband, 26 U.S.C. sec.1402(a) (8)(a). In order to rebut this presumption, a wife must exercise "substantially all of the management and control" of the business.

  The intent of the law is to prevent a double tax. The effect for women (and compounded by exemptions in the Equal Credit Opportunity Act regarding community property jurisdictions) is that, the presumption may act as an obstacle to successful business ownership.

- The social security system, financed through direct payroll taxation, was established in the 1930's to protect Americans against risks to economic security: death, disability, and retirement of a breadwinner. Through the years, social security laws have been amended to accomodate the times. However, as Congressional hearings and legal analyses point out, women business owners, along with working women and two-earner couples in general, are presently inadequately served by the social security system. Shortcomings include:

  - failure of the system to continue protection for women whose wage earning careers are interspersed with work in the home

  - married couples, earning two salaries, must choose to receive benefits based upon just one of the salaries; no credit is given for the social security tax contributions of the spouse

  - inadequate protection for lesser earning divorced spouses

  - inadequate benefits for lesser earning widowed spouses.

One issue regarding the tax treatment of women business owners which was recently eliminated deserves explanation. Several publications pre-dating the Economic Recovery Tax Act of 1981 took issue with an estate tax provision dubbed the "widow's tax" (26 U.S.C. 2040). The tax detrimentally affected women who owned businesses or farms jointly with their husbands. The Tax Code assessed estate taxes on the value of the entire jointly owned business upon the first death of one of the spouses. The surviving spouse could only diminish this onerous tax burden to the extent that acquisitions of and capital additions to the family business could be proven to have been furnished in "money or money's worth" (as per the 1954 Code) or "material participation" (as per the 1978 Code amendments 26 U.S.C. 2040 [c]) by that surviving spouse.

While the statutory construction was gender neutral, in effect, widows were more frequently assessed the tax than were widowers. Women, generally on the lower end of the income scale, do not commonly contribute to the purchase and maintenance of family-owned businesses in "money"; their "domestic" services could not be included as "material participation"; and other participation in the family enterprise was frequently under-documented. Consequently, surviving widows were too often forced to sell their family businesses or farms in order to satisfy the estate taxes imposed on the estate of their deceased husbands. (For extensive analysis and discussion of the "widow's tax" see U.S. Senate, 97th Congress, 1st session: Major Estate and Gift Tax Issues, Hearings before the Subcommittee on Estate and Gift Taxation of the Committee on Finance, Washington, D.C. vol. 1 May 1, 1981 and vol. 2 June 5, 1981.)

With the passage of the Economic Recovery Tax Act of 1981, Code Section 2040(c) was repealed and amendments to the interspousal gift tax and marital deductions laws (26 U.S.C. 2056) have supplanted its function. Now, each spouse owns one-half of all jointly-owned property including family-owned businesses, regardless of which spouse furnished the money or services for its acquisition. In addition, the quantitative ceilings on lifetime and deathtime transfers between spouses have been removed. Husbands and wives are not assessed taxes on their gifts to one another, regardless of the value of the gifts. Therefore, utilizing the unlimited marital deduction and unlimited gift tax, surviving spouses can eliminate all tax liability of the deceased spouses' estate.

It is cautioned, however, that for all marital property, the tax laws are most beneficial when the marital deduction is only used to the extent that it reduces the decedent's estate taxes to zero. Beyond this point, greatly increased tax liability may be experienced when the surviving spouse subsequently transfers the business. To spouses owning a business, these considerations should be carefully examined with regard to the feasibility of eventual transfers of the business by the surviving spouse to children or outside purchasers.

Another tax-related issue involves the membership practices of private clubs. Business is frequently conducted outside the parameters defined as "the workspace." In this regard, membership in private clubs is frequently identified as a valuable arena for establishing business associations. In fact, it is not uncommon for members of private clubs to claim a business tax deduction for the costs of membership and attendance.

A legal issue of importance to women business owners arises in this context in that many private clubs exclude women (as well as blacks or other minorities) from membership or participation. Due to their private nature, the activities of private clubs are not subject to regulation under the 1964 Civil Rights Act. However, case law and scholarly debate takes issue with discriminatory policies of private business clubs:

If the activities of a private club are truly personal and social, rather than commercial, then members should not be able to claim a business tax deduction for them. Conversely, if the activities of a private club are substantially commercial, then the members should be subject to the same nondiscrimation laws that govern other commercial activities in our society. (Personal Viewpoint by Brooksley Born, The American Bar Association Journal (August 1982): 1024.)

In 1980, the American Bar Association adopted a resolution to urge Congress to apply the Civil Rights Act to "public accommodation" business clubs that derive substantial incomes from business sources. Congressional action has not yet been taken on the resolution and the debate continues. (For additional information, see: ABA Journal (August 1982): 884 and 1024, case law indexed under "Private Clubs".)

Citations

The following citations are limited to those publications which address tax consequences specifically pertinent to women business owners. General analysis of the Economic Recovery Tax Act is not included as it does not directly focus on the widow's tax or women business owners.

Hall, Cynthia Holcomb. "The Working Woman and the Federal Income Tax." American Bar Association Journal 61 (1975): 716.

The article provides a historical perspective and explanations of provisions of the Tax Code (of 1975) which are specifically pertinent to women who work outside the home. The author analyzes: community property as contrasted to common law tax provisions (including the origins of joint tax returns); child care as a business deduction; the middle-income bias; tax benefits to single heads of households: and alimony and child support provisions.

Oates, Hugh F., Jr. "Tax--Only God Knows For Sure But the IRS Makes a Good Guess--Tables." North Carolina Law Review 53 (1976): 161-169.

The author reviews disagreement in the courts as to whether tax liability should be based on actual or on actuarial life expectancy. The author accepts the "actuarial fact" that women outlive men. The pertinence of this article rests in its analysis of case law controversies surrounding the use of actuarial tables in general and from the inception of their inclusion in the Tax Code.

President's Interagency Task Force on Women Business Owners. The Bottom Line: Unequal Enterprise in America. Washington, D.C.: U.S. Government Printing Office, 1978.

The report contains a brief discussion of the structure and distribution of women-owned small businesses highlighting the direct effects of: (1) the "widow's" estate tax (26 I.R.C. section 2040) and (2) tax treatment in community property states--there is a statutory presumption in the Internal Revenue Code (26 U.S.C section 1402(a)(5)(A)) that husbands in community property states are the sole owners of family businesses.

Wives must exercise "substantially all of the management and control" of a family business to rebut the ownership presumption. As a consequence, women face greater difficulty in establishing their ownership and credit histories. Thereby women are further deterred from forming business enterprises.

Roff, Douglas E. "Gender Based Mortality Tables and the Code: An Equal Protection Analysis." University of Florida Law Review 33 (1980): 122.

The use of gender-based mortality tables in the Internal Revenue Code for determining income, estate and gift tax liability is challenged as a violation of the constitutional guarantees of due process and equal protection under the law.

The effects of gender-based tax tables on life insurance annuities (IRC section 72 Reg. section 1.72) and charitable remainder trusts prove burdensome to women. In one case, tax consequences of revisionary trusts (IRC section 2512), women receive slightly favored treatment.

For example, an individual tax-payer purchases life insurance anticipating a return on that investment at a future date, e.g. age 66. As that return is actualized, the taxpayer must include the portion of that return which represents income from the investment in taxable income. The portion representing a mere recovery on the principal investment may be excluded from taxable income. Depending on the taxpayer's life expectancy, a ratio of inclusion to exclusion from taxable income is applied by the IRC. The longer the life expectancy, the longer it will take to fully recover the principal investment. On an annual basis, a taxpayer with a long life expectancy will be assessed taxes such that the principal return is small and the taxable income large. Conversely, a shorter life expectancy results in smaller taxable income. Once an annuity is purchased, the IRC ratio is established and never changed. Premature death causes no tax loss and outlived life expectancy results in additional tax and economic benefits.

The IRC classifies all taxpayers by gender in reliance on the actuarial assumption that women outlive men by five years. Roff says: "The result of this policy is that women who are similarly situated to men with respect to age and economic status will have more burdensome tax consequences based solely on an accident of birth."

The author traces the development of the standard of judicial scrutiny applied to gender-based classifications by the Supreme Court. Applying the "middle-tier test", the author draws the following conclusions:

- the administrative convenience of using gender-based tables is outweighed by their inaccuracy

- more accurate indicators of life expectancy, such as health characteristics, are readily available

- the class-wide generalizations based on gender result in substantial and significant burdens to a high percentage of individual women, i.e., many women do not outlive all men. Analogizing from the Court's decisions in Craig v. Boren and Manhart (see the section on insurance issues), the author concludes:

> "In light of the emphasis the Court has placed on the role of individual rights in the gender area, a classification as patently overboard and over inclusive as this cannot be sustained."

Discussion of alternatives to the use of gender-based tax tables suggest: the return to the use of gender-neutral tables; or, the use of health-related characteristics in estimating life expectancy and tax liability.

U.S. Commission on Civil Rights. Sex Bias in the United States Code. Washington, D.C.: 1977.

The report identifies and analyzes gender-based references in the United States Code. The bulk of the report is a title-by-title review limited to the identification of bias in the terminology of the Code.

However, regarding bias in Title 26, the Internal Revenue Code, the report does identify the substantive bias in presuming all gross income and deductions of a family-owned business in a community property state to be uniquely attributed to the husband, unless the wife exercises substantially all the management and control. The analysis recognizes the benign purpose of the provision but recommends that:

> The provision might be recast to state that the gross income and deductions shall be attributed to the spouse who in fact exercises dominant control of the business.

U.S. Department of the Treasury Study Team. Credit & Capital Formation. Report to the President's Interagency Task Force on Women Business Owners. Washington, D.C.: 1978.

Working from the standpoint that,"taxation is not sex-specific," the study provides a thorough explanation of the structure of small business taxation including: forms of organization; the distribution of women-owned businesses among the forms (sole proprietorships (98 percent), partnerships (1.7 percent), and corporations (0.3 percent); tax provisions (amortization, early year's payments, payroll taxes, and retirement); Employee Retirement Insurance Act (ERISA) and owner's security; 1978 proposed legislation (additional graduation of corporate taxes, depreciation and simplification of the asset depreciation range (ADR), depreciation amounts and time periods, investment tax credit, new jobs incentive); and taxation to encourage venture capital.

There is discussion of the "widow's tax" which, "contains no structural bias against women business owners as compared to other business owners," but may "as a practical matter" raise problems for surviving wives whose contributions to the acquisitions of family owned businesses are inadequately documented and thereby suffer onerous estate taxes upon the death of their joint-owner husbands.

The study team concludes that it is appropriate for family-owned businesses to be conducted on the same bases as other small business: "the answer to the problem is not to create special rules for spouses," but rather, the study team strongly recommends the dissemination of estate tax information to wives whose contributions to family-owned businesses may be inadequately documented.

Insurance

The importance to small businesses of obtaining adequate and appropriate insurance coverage cannot be overstated. Small businesses often function on closely watched budgets and have little hope of absorbing the costly effects of loss or damage due to theft, physical disaster or legal entanglements.

Commercial insurance is generally in the form of property and liability insurance policies. In addition, the small business owner, as an individual, may be advised and even required (as collateral for business loans) to carry health (medical and disability), and life insurance policies. Therefore women business owners are adjudged insurance risk-worthy both as business owners and as women.

Numerous studies of insurance practices conducted by state commissions on the status of women and interest groups, as well as the findings of recent state and federal litigation, indicate that women face disparate treatment in all phases of the insurance industry.

For example, a married woman may be denied life insurance terms and conditions that are offered to similarly situated men: while a man may receive a waiver of premium of up to $150,000, a similarly situated woman would only receive a $50,000 waiver.

Terms and conditions of health and disability insurance polices frequently deny coverage to women for maternity-related expenses while coverage is offered to men for even "voluntary" gender-related medical treatment.

Underwriting policies, the selection of insurable risks, may result in the denial of property insurance to married women whose husbands do not cosign the insurance policy. There is some indication that due to underwriting policies, women business owners are not targeted for commercial insurance coverage.

A third example, an issue of state and federal litigation, is of discrimination evidenced in the rate structure and premiums applied throughout the insurance industry. Life expectancy tables used in determining life insurance rates show women to outlive men. While this may be a valid statistical measure, the resultant generalization is not true on a high percentage of individual females who do not in fact outlive similarly situated males.

Judicial Review

At the state level, litigative efforts have been directed toward holding both state insurance commissioners and the private insurance companies liable under 42 U.S.C. sections 1983 and 1985 for depriving or conspiring to deprive women of their civil rights.

Litigation concerning sex discrimination in insurance which has received federal court attention has focused on violations of employment discrimination laws (Title VII of the Civil Rights Act of 1964) and the Constitutional guarantees of due process and equal protection under the law. Title VII prohibits employers from discriminating based on race, color, religion, sex or national origin, "in any way which would deprive any individual of employment opportunities or otherwise adversely affect his status as an employee." [42 U.S.C. section 2000e(a)(2)]

Litigation of two insurance practices has reached the attention of the United States Supreme Court:

● Disability coverage for pregnancy - Insurance practices have not been found to be in violation of Title VII. (See Geduldig v. Aiello, 417 U.S. 484 (1974); General Electric Co. v. Gilbert, 429 U.S. 125 (1976); and Nashville Gas Co. v. Satty, 434 U.S. 136 (1977)) Note however, that congressional action has since prohibited sex discrimination in disability insurance coverage.

● Life insurance coverage of employee pension plans - Pension plans, utilizing gender-based life expectancy tables and thereby requiring female employees to pay higher premiums than male employees receiving the same insurance coverage, have been found to be in violation of Title VII. (See Manhart v. City of Los Angeles Water and Power 435 U.S. 702, 55 L Ed 2nd 98 Section 1370 (1978)). One case currently before the Supreme Court, (Arizona Governing Committee v. Norris 671 F. 2d. 330, 486 F. Supp. 645 (1981), cert. granted October 12, 1982), also involves pension plans which rely on gender-based life expectancy tables. In Norris female and male employees pay the same premiums but the benefits women employees receive are less than those received by the men. The Supreme Court decided this was a violation of Title VII (103 Sct. 3492 (1983) 463 U.S. 1073 (1983))

Legislative Action

In 1945, Congress passed the McCarran-Ferguson Insurance Regulation Act (15 U.S.C. sections 1011-1015 (1945)). It provides that "the business of insurance" is subject to state regulation and is generally exempt from federal antitrust law. However, federal laws which specifically address the business of insurance do supercede state regulations. The Act has been invoked by the insurance industry in resisting federal regulation, and, for the most part regulation of the insurance industry remains on the state level.

Many states do statutorily prohibit discriminatory practices of insurance companies. However, standard provisions merely regulate "unfair discrimination." Traditional insurance concepts are used in defining "unfair discrimination" such that the practices outlined above are permitted as based upon legitimate class, life expectancy and degree of risk factors.

Federal legislation aimed at eliminating sex and race discrimination in insurance has been reviewed in both the House of Representatives and the Senate, i.e., The Non discrimination in Insurance Acts. Because this legislation would specifically focus on the business of insurance, it would be in compliance with the McCarran-Ferguson Act. Public interest, civil and women's rights organizations voice strong support for the proposed antidiscrimination legislation. In contrast, the insurance industry is greatly opposed to federal regulation of any kind. No legislative action had been taken at the time of publication of this bibliography.

Research and analysis of commercial insurance coverage available to women business owners is greatly lacking. Just one publication, The President's Interagency Task Force on Women Business Owners' Report, The Bottom Line (previously cited), attempts to examine the legal context and to describe a limited study of the practical effects of commercial insurance regulation (or lack thereof) for women entrepreneurs.

On the other hand, much attention is being given to legal and theoretical issues pertinent to every woman's access to fair and adequate insurance coverage. Because most women entrepreneurs are sole proprietors, who are assessed risk-worthiness based on their classification as women, it is of utmost importance to women business owners that life, health and property insurance not discriminate on the basis of gender. Moreover, the monetary value of life and health insurance policies is significant in that they may be required as, and applied toward, collateral on business loans.

Citations

The following citations identify some of the most recent and comprehensive analyses of insurance issues pertinent to women business owners. The list is not exhaustive with regard to publications on individual and pension insurance policies but does highlight major sources of information and those which specifically focus on the availability of commercial insurance to women entrepreneurs.

Because much of insurance regulation occurs at the state level, extremely valuable primary sources of information are the state regulatory authorities (reports of the individual state authorities are not listed in this bibliography). State commissioners or directors of insurance are excellent sources of information regarding the most recent legal developments as well as for reports on discriminatory insurance practices in individual states.

"Challenges to Sex-Based Mortality Tables in Insurance and Pensions".
Women's Rights Law Reporter (Fall/Winter 1979-80): 59.

This article presents a thorough examination of the derivation and use of gender-based tables in all forms of insurance and a comprehensive description of state and federal regulatory measures and litigation.

The historical perspective on the use of gender-based mortality tables contains an interesting comparison of the statistical validity of modern tables developed by the Society of Actuaries. The 1958 Commissioners' Standard Ordinary (CSO) table and a 1979 proposed replacement are carefully described. The CSO table, which is used throughout the insurance industry, is criticized for its reliance on "setback" rather than actual data on female and male life expectancies.

Inconsistencies in the use of gender-based tables amplify the disparate effects women face in insurance. For example, in group life insurance, where women would benefit from the use of gender-based mortality tables, they are not used. Neutral tables are. Thus, women pay higher premiums. In group annuities, where men benefit from gender-based mortality tables, these tables are used.

State regulation of insurance is found to vary greatly by state. State statutes prohibiting discrimination based on sex and marital status focus primarily on "expanding the availability of coverage and ensuring equality of terms and conditions in policies." A 1979 model regulation of the National Association of Insurance Commissioners and the Unfair Insurance Trade Practice Act, has provided some impetus for state adoption of antidiscriminatory underwriting restrictions. However, continued reliance on gender-based tables and overbroad and misleading language of "unfair discrimination" permit discrimination to continue.

Litigation on the state level has resulted in state insurance commissioners being found liable under 42 U.S.C., sections 1983 and 1985(c), of depriving or conspiring to deprive women of their civil rights by failing to disapprove discriminatory insurance policies. Case law indicates that insurance companies may not be liable as conspirators under cover of state law, (42 U.S.C section 1983), but are as conspirators under 42 U.S.C section 1985. "Actual justification," a valid defense in lower court cases, is an issue which had not yet reached the Supreme Court.

The article concludes with a discussion of the federal laws and their implications in L.A. Department of Water and Power v. Manhart.

Key, Sidney J. "Sex-Based Pension Plans in Perspective: City of Los Angeles Department of Water and Power v. Manhart". Harvard Women's Law Journal (Spring 1979): 1-47.

The article examines the correlation between gender and mortality rates and the statistical usefulness of gender-based mortality tables to pension plans. The main focus is on Title VII and the Manhart decision. However, also included is an analysis of the extension of Manhart to non-employee related insurance practices. The author examines the conflict inherent in social policy considerations.

A description of litigation challenging gender-based private insurance policies based on the Equal Protection Clause of the 14th Amendment, sections 1983 and 1985 of the Civil Rights Act of 1871 and state equal rights amendments is provided:

State insurance laws were amended in two states, Pennsylvania and New York, pending two cases: Stern v. Massachusettes Indemnity and Life Insurance Company, 365 F. Supp 433 (E.D. Pa. 1973), a claim based on 1983; and Gilpin v. Schenck, Civ 420 (S.D.N.Y. filed Jan. 24, 1974), an equal protection claim.

A number of 42 U.S.C. sec. 1983 sex discrimination claims have been dismissed for failure to establish state action as defined in Jackson v. Metropolitan Edison Company, 419 U.S. 345 (1975) e.g. Broderick v. Association of Hospital Services of Philadelphia, 536 F. 2d 1, 2 (3rd Cir. 1976); Madison v. Keyston Insurance Company, No. 77-2559 (E.D. Pa. Sept. 21, 1978); Reichart v. Payne, 396 F. Supp. 1010 (N.D. Cal. 1975), 591 F. 2d 499 (9th Cir. 1979).

The author concludes that the primary impact of this litigation has been to cause prompt changes in state regulations regarding sex discrimination in insurance.

Naierman, Naomi, Ruth Brannon and Beverly Wahl. Sex Discrimination in Insurance: A Guide for Women. Women's Equity Action League, Washington, D.C.: n.d.

A popular brochure defining discrimination in the insurance industry and describing its manifestations in disability, health, life, property and liability insurance. Also provided is an overview of legal challenges of the discrimination made on the state and federal levels; comprehensive bibliographic references to pertinent research by state commissions including lists of State Regulatory Authorities and State Commissions for Women; proposed avenues for further action including specific improvements to regulations, consumer lobbying efforts, health maintenance organizations (HMO's), alternatives to existing plans, national health insurance legislation and the Equal Rights Amendment.

Sydlaski, Janet. "Comment: Gender Classifications in the Insurance Industry." Columbia Law Review 75 (1975): 1381-1403.

The author acknowledges the effects of gender discrimination in property and casualty insurance but defers discussion thereof to other publications. The article focuses on individual disability and medical insurance: the problems, an equal protection analysis thereof, discussion of industry rationale, and posits state and federal remedies.

U.S. Commission on Civil Rights. Discrimination Against Minorities and Women in Pensions and Life and Disability Insurance. (Vol. 1, Proceedings and Papers, Vol. 2, Exhibits.) Washington, D.C.: U.S. Government Printing Office, 1978.

In 1978 the Civil Rights Commission conducted a consultation drawing together the foremost experts from throughout the nation in the fields of pensions and life and disability insurance. This two-volume publication is a compilation of documents, research and position papers presented to the consultation and the ensuing statements and dialogue thereon. Participants included experts from within the insurance industry, state insurance commissioners, public interest analysts, academicians, actuaries and statisticians, and legal experts. The report is an invaluable source of information concerning discrimination in the insurance industry.

U.S. Congress. House. Committee on Commerce, Transportation and Tourism. Non-Discrimination in Insurance Act of 1983 (H.R. 100)." 98th Congress, 1st session, 1983. Serial 98-35.

The focus of the hearing was on gender-based discrimination. Many public interest groups and representatives of the insurance industry testified.

_____. Subcommittee on Energy and Commerce. Hearing on the Nondiscrimination in Insurance Act of 1981. 97th Congress, 1st session, 1981. Serial 97-22.

The purpose of the proposed legislation was to eliminate discrimination based on race, color, religion, sex and national origin in all phases of insurance and annuities, i.e., access to and availability of coverage; underwriting terms, conditions and rates; and benefits and requirements of the contracts and methods used in their determination. The major focus of the hearing is on sex discrimination prohibitions including the use of gender-based rate tables. The Act would establish a private right of action in Federal Court for individuals seeking relief from discriminatory treatment, after exhaustion of state judicial and administrative remedies. At the time of the hearing, the bill was supported by over 85 members of the House.

The publication includes the statements of several congressional sponsors and committee members addressing the benefits and criticism of federal insurance regulation. Honorable John D. Dingel provides a comprehensive analysis of the policy issues and arguments pertaining to the proposed legislation, incidence of discrimination against women in insurance and annuities, and a rebuttal to insurance industry arguments: (1) McCarran-Ferguson does not prohibit Federal regulation; (2) life expectancy does not justify gender classifications just as it would not justify religious or racial classifications; (3) changing health, stress and behavioral characteristics have greater statistical importance than does gender [refers to Dr. Ingrid Waldron, "An Analysis of Causes of Sex Differences in Morbidity and Mortality" (Sixth Vanderbilt University Conference on Frontiers of Sociology) and Waldron, "Why Do Women Live Longer Than Men", Journal of Human Stress vol.2 (Mar 1978) and ibid., Part II (June 1976)]; (4) the insurance industry distorts the averages of men's and women's mortality; (5) judicial scrutiny rejects classifications as discriminatory to individuals; (6) state regulation is inadequate; (7) actuarial tables are based on an arbitrary "setback"; and (8) the "cost impact" argument of the insurance industry is an exaggeration of the actual costs of changing to gender neutral tables.

Statements by public interest groups and the insurance industry probe the issues in depth. Of special note to women business owners is the mention of sex discrimination in commercial insurance by Judy Schub of the National Federation of Business and Professional Women's Clubs. The author draws parallels between discrimination in insurance and in credit.

U.S. Congress. Senate. Committee on the Judiciary. Subcommittee on Antitrust, Monopoly and Business Rights. Non-discrimination in Insurance Act (S.2477). 96th Congress, 2nd session, 1980. Serial 96-80.

The purpose of the proposed legislation is to prohibit discrimination on the basis of race, color, religion, sex or national origin in the sale, under-writing and rating of all insurance (similar to H.R. 100 introduced by Representative John Dingell in 1979). Senator Metzenbaum summarizes the issue in his introductory statement to the hearing as follows:

Many persons in the insurance industry claim that the use of sex as a classification is just an actuarial question. If statistics show an aggregate difference by sex, they say, leave it to the actuaries to set the prices.

I disagree. To disadvantage an entire class of persons as a result of an immutable characteristic over which they have no control raises fundamental questions of public policy. Issues of such magnitude should be decided by the public's elected representatives, not left to technical experts employed by insurance companies.

_____. Committee on Labor and Human Resources. Subcommittee on Labor. Hearing to consider the Retirement Equity Act of 1983 (S.191). 98th Congress, 1st session, October 4, 1983.

_____. Committee on Commerce, Science and Transportation. Hearing to consider the Fair Insurance Practice Act (S.2204). 97th Congress, 2nd session, 1982. Serial 97-137.

Witnesses included Mary Gray, President of The Women's Equity Action League and Gaye Melich, Executive Director of the National Women's Political Caucus. Examples of sex discrimination in insurance were discussed.

_____. Committee on Commerce, Science and Transportation. Hearing to Consider the Fair Insurance Practices Act (S. 372). 98th Congress, 1st session, 1983. Serial 98-34.

Proposed Act prohibits discrimination in writing and selling insurance (including annuity and pension contracts) on the basis of race, color, religion, national orgin or sex. The focus of the hearing was on gender-based discrimination.

U.S. Department of the Treasury Study Team. Credit and Capital Formation: a Report to the President's Interagency Task Force on Women Business Owners. (April 1978) 19-24. Available for review, Library, U.S. Small Business Administration, Washington, D.C.

While this early research is limited to reliance on small, informal sampling surveys, the study's specific focus on women in business provides a useful foundation for future research.

The chapter describes the profound importance of insurance (security bonds and property and liability insurance) to small businesses and examines the incidence of discrimination against women business owners.

The study team's survey of six surety companies revealed no explicitly stated bias against women business owners, but that reliance is placed on the "three C's of character, capacity and capital", and the business track record compiled by surety underwriters.

Sureties rarely underwrite small business firms. Referring to a 1979 North Carolina report on insurance, the study team states that while discrimination based on sex does not affect the rates of commercial insurance (which is the result of the expense factor, the agents commission, and the loss factor, based on projected claims), it is "an integral factor determining eligibility" (emphasis added). A study team survey of commercial agents/brokers throughout the United States revealed that women-owned businesses were not deemed a "viable segment of the business community," and were not a targeted market for policy coverage.

Discriminatory provisions of income and medical insurance, although "ancillary costs of doing business," are examined in detail due to their profound importance to the economic status of all women.

The study team concludes that denial of equal access to insurance at fair rates affects the economic status of all women. It touches employment discrimination, opportunities to hold a job, ability to maintain a family in the face of personal catastrophe, and economic security. Other economic disadvantages of women can be magnified by discriminatory, inadequate, or prohibitively costly insurance.

The study team concludes its discussion of insurance by examining the viability of federal regulation of insurance in light of the McCarran-Ferguson Act and the public interest.

The publications contain testimony and reports by public interest groups and the insurance industry.

Property

Property and contract issues arise for women business owners when their rights to own, manage, control, and convey personal or real property are constrained. For the most part, women in business, and otherwise, may freely exercise these important rights. However, vestiges of restraints on women's property rights remain from European and British legal tradition.

Property laws in 41 states grew out of the English common law system in which the occurrence of marriage brought on the total restraint of women's rights to own, control, or convey marital or separately owned property. Husbands' and wives' earnings remained in their separate ownership but only the husband had the right to control his own and his wife's property. As Blackstone described:

> the very being or legal existence of the woman is suspended during the marriage, or at least is incorporated and consolidated into that of the husband.

The remaining nine states evolved community property systems, based upon the Spanish or French (Napoleonic) tradition. In these states, property acquired by either spouse during marriage was equally shared, in regard to ownership, by both spouses. A shortcoming arose however, where the rights to control and manage community property remained vested solely in the husband.

In the early 19th century most of these restraints on women's property rights were statutorily removed by state adoption of the Married Women's Property Acts. The Acts enabled married women to own, manage and convey real and personal property. Both husband and wife were then free from liability on their spouse's separate debts.

Unfortunately, in a dozen states, vestiges of the discriminatory traditional common law and community property systems still remain. Not until 1975 did California remove the statutory assumption that community property management and control was the sole domain of the husband. Research published as recently as 1978 reveals that in Texas, the husband had the sole power to convey real and personal property; in Louisiana, the husband may still convey real property alone unless it is specifically in his wife's name.

Thus, in some states women business owners could still find themselves in situations where their hard-earned assets could be transferred away without their consent. The importance of establishing control over separate and marital property should also be considered in conjunction with estate and gift tax laws and the Equal Credit Opportunity Act (see discussions in relevant sections of this bibliography).

In a few states (California, Florida, Nevada, Pennsylvania and Texas), legal technicalities still require married women to petition the state, making a case for the removal of common law disabilities on their rights to engage in business. Similarly some states either require women owners to file records of their separate business assets, or enable them to do so, in order to protect these assets from husbands' liabilities and creditors.

Much of the research on women's property rights was conducted prior to 1978 and in conjunction with actions undertaken in observance of the United Nations Decade for Women (1975-1985). During 1975, International Women's Year (IWY), state level surveys were conducted by state commissions on the status of women, identifying the existence of discriminatory property laws. Although the studies are entitled "The Legal Status of Homemakers in...[a particular state]," the actual focus of the publications is on legal impediments to married women's property rights, including the right to engage in business.

In 1981, the White House Task Force on the 50 States Project was charged by the President to conduct a state-by-state survey of laws affecting women's rights and opportunities. Unfortunately, the 50 States Project is only as thorough as the state level data it compiles; while some states submitted insightful analyses of their laws, others merely described linguistic bias, and several states did not respond at all to the Task Force survey.

Apart from IWY-stimulated surveys of the law, and general discussions in legal textbooks, little analysis exists that examines the actual effects of state or federal laws on women's rights to freely own, manage and convey separate and marital property and to engage in business. Several publications merely describe linguistic bias in state and federal laws.

Citations

The publications cited in this section provide a sampling of scholarly analysis in this area, instructional texts and guides for the layperson. Many of the publications survey the legal status of all women regarding an array of legal issues. These contents are mentioned here along with the property and contract issues which are of special importance to women entrepreneurs.

> (Name of State) Commission on Status of Women. "The Legal Status of Homemakers in (State)." Out of print. Superintendent of Documents, Government Printing Office (1978).

In 1977, as part of the observance of the UN-declared International Women's Decade, state commissions on the status of women compiled information on discrimination against married women in property and contract laws. Each publication details the rights and restrictions important to women under the laws of the particular state.

Alexander, Shana and Barbara Brudno. State by State Guide to Women's
    Legal Rights. Los Angeles: Wollstonecraft Inc., 1975.

A popular guide to the rights of women with regard to: marriage, children,
divorce, rape, widowhood, work, crime, age, and citizenship. A helpful
glossary of legal terms is also included.

A glance at the state-by-state analysis of marriage rights immediately reveals basic encumbrances on women's contractual rights. For example, in
Kentucky a married woman's rights are described as follows:

> Rights of Wife: Generally, wife may enter into contracts and engage in
> business on the same basis as her husband, but she may not contract to
> guarantee her husband's debts and she may not sell property unless her
> husband joins her in the deed--a restriction not placed on the husband.

Babcock, Barbara, Ann Freedman, Eleanor Holmes Norton and Susan Ross.
    Sex Discrimination and the Law, Causes and Remedies. Boston: Little,
    Brown and Co., 1975. (Supplement by Wendy Williams 1978).

A comprehensive scholarly text providing pertinent case law, legislation,
articles; historical, economic and sociological materials; comments, questions and analysis of sex discrimination. The chapters provide detailed
insights into: Constitutional Law and Feminist Theory, Employment Discrimination, Family Law, Criminal Law, Reproductive Freedom, Education, and Equal
Access to Public Accomodations.

Kay, Herma Hill. Text, Cases and Materials on Sex-Based Discrimination.
    Minnesota: West Publishing Co., 1981. (Supplement by Kay, 1983)

A casebook on sex discrimination examining: constitutional limits, interaction within the family, and discrimination in employment, education and
criminal law.

Regarding property rights of married women, the text includes the case of
Kirchberg v. Feenstra, 101 S. CT 1195, 65 L.Ed 2d 428 (U.S. Supreme Court
1981), in which a husband's unilateral right as "head and master" to dispose
of community property in Louisiana was held to violate the Equal Protection
Clause of the 14th Amendment.

DeCrow, Karen. Sexist Justice. New York: Random House, 1974.

An early but very thorough publication examining incidences of sex discrimination in the United States. The following areas are described in detail: A
study of misogyny, the 14th Amendment, the Federal Government, money and
employment--fair representation and the job market, credit, estate law,
family law, criminal law, motherhood and abortion, education, and the Equal
Rights Amendment.

Within the discussion of family law, the author describes legal restrictions in various states on a married woman's contractual rights and her rights to engage in business:

Laws in ten states still restrict a married woman's contractual rights (Alabama, Arizona, California, Florida, Georgia, Idaho, Indiana, Kentucky, Nevada, and North Carolina). In four states (California, Florida, Nevada, and Pennsylvania), a wife must obtain court approval before she can engage in an independent business. The Florida law requires her to file a petition stating her character, habits, education, mental capacities, and the reasons why the judge should grant her request. In New York, a woman who wishes to get a license from the Alcohol Beverage Control Board to run a restaurant or bar, must have a male co-signer for the license. (A man applying for the same license does not need the co-signature of a woman.)

In Kentucky, a woman is generally barred from co-signing a loan without her husband. In Georgia, she cannot use her property as collateral for a loan. In Alabama, Florida, Indiana, North Carolina, and Texas, she cannot dispose of her property without her husband's consent.

Francis, Philip. Legal Status of Women. Dobbs Ferry, N.Y.: Oceana Publications, 1978.

An investigation into the status of women's rights in the following areas: marriage, abortion, contracts and debts, property rights and inheritance, divorce, employment, and crime.

Regarding Contracts and Debts, findings of particular interest to women business owners include:

- a historical perspective of women's legal right to contract discussing common law restraints and subsequent statutory restoration of contractual rights.

- a state-by-state explanation of the varying degrees of contractual rights women enjoy regarding:

  (1) interspousal contracts--a wife and husband may contract freely with each other in 18 states, are prohibited to do so in two states, and face various restrictions (described in the text) in the balance of the states; (2) conveyances of real property--a wife may convey her real property, unrestrained, as if she were unmarried in 25 states, but must be joined by her husband in eight states (Alabama, Florida, Indiana, Kentucky, North Carolina, Ohio, Pennsylvania, Texas); (3) transfers of personal property--a wife may feely transfer her personal property in all but three states (Georgia, North Carolina, Texas).

- a discussion of a woman's rights to engage in her own separate business: Most states do have statutory enactments providing for wives to freely engage in business, however five states technically require wives to formally petition for removal of the common law restraints

(California, Florida, Nevada, Pennsylvania, Texas). Neither spouse is liable for the separate debts of the other. In Massachusetts a wife must file a business certificate to protect her business against her husband's creditors. Seven states permit each spouse to make a public record of separately owned property (Alaska, California, Indiana, Missouri, Nevada, Oklahoma, South Dakota). In two states, (California, Nevada) if a husband's investment in his wife's business exceeds $500 or if he assists in its management, the wife may lose the statutory protection. The distinctions are drawn between a wife's earnings in community property states versus common-law states

- the assignment of wages earned by one spouse to pay creditors of the other spouse must be in writing in 16 states, but is only required of a husband's assenting to pay his wife's creditors (not vice versa) in nine states (Alaska, Indiana, Louisiana, Massachusetts, Minnesota, Missouri, Texas, Wisconsin, Wyoming).

- an explanation of real and personal property exempt from seizure to satisfy personal debts. Specific inquiry into "Homestead Laws", i.e., which safeguard the family home and property against debtors, reveals that 30 states provide the exemption to the "head of the family"--11 states provide it to property owners regardless of "head of family" status and the remaining states vary in their application of homestead laws (details in text)

- a brief overview of women and credit looks into the impetus for the Equal Credit Opportunity Act (ECOA); findings specifically pertinent to women business owners include: a brief historical view of a wife's rights to own and convey property; and an explanation of jointly owned property in common law states, (where property acquired during marriage is assumed to be under the management and control of the husband under three forms of joint ownership: tenancy by the entirety, tenancy in common, and joint tenancy

- the distinction between property held in community property jurisdictions (Arizona, California, Indiana, Nevada, New Mexico, Texas, Washington) where the husband, as head of the community, has the duty to manage marital property for the benefit of his wife and family. Generally, the wife does not have the right to control community property and may not contract debts chargeable against it.

- inheritance rights of dower, curtesy and election are described with a state-by-state explanation of statutory inheritance provisions.

Hemphill, Anita and Charles Hemphill, Jr. Womenlaw: a Guide to Legal Matters Vital to Women. Englewood Cliffs, N.J.: Prentice-Hall: 1981.

An informative publication designed to provide the layperson with an understanding of aspects of the law which primarily concern women, or treat men and women differently. Chapters focus on legal aspects of: marriage, domicile, adoption and guardianship, battered women, abortion, birth control and sterilization, rape, children, cohabitation, dissolution of marriage, job discrimination, widowhood, benefits, access to legal help; and, of particular interest to women business owners, credit and property rights.

The distinctions between community property and common law systems are explained in conjunction with the three forms of joint ownership: joint tenancy, tenancy by the entirety and tenancy in common. Shortcomings of the Married Women's Property Acts, enabling married women to "retain the profits, rents, dividends, or other income from her separate property" are briefly mentioned. For example: several states prohibit a married woman from contracting to sell or lease her individual real estate without her husband's written permission.

The discussion of credit provides a brief explanation of the guarantees under the Equal Credit Opportunity Act (ECOA).

Kanowitz, Leo. Sex Roles in Law and Society, Cases and Materials. University of New Mexico Press: 1973. (Supplement, 1974).

An early casebook examining sex discrimination and the law in the United States. Contains court decisions, statutory enactments and analysis of the law's traditional view of sex roles, marital status, employment, constitutional law, the media, pornography, sexual preference and appearance.

The book contains analysis of a statute enacted in 1973 in New Mexico which specified that commercial or business community property was presumptively managed and controlled by the husband. To overcome this presumption a wife was required to file a written statement with the county clerk. (N.M. Rev. Stats. section 57-4A-71).

Lynch, Jane S. and Sara L. Smith. The Woman's Guide to Legal Rights. Chicago: Contemporary Books, 1979.

A helpful guide for the layperson providing practical advice and explanations of legal issues regarding: the home and family, employment, the marketplace, and crimes against women. The authors use examples and a question-and-answer format.

White House Task Force. The 50 States Project: Status of Women. Washington, D.C. (Not yet published. For information contact: The Office of Public Liaison, The White House, Washington, D.C.).

A state-by-state review of sex discrimination in the state codes as analyzed by appointees of the 50 state governors and compiled by the White House Task Force from 1981-1983. Some states look to the effects of state laws on women's rights while others restrict the survey to incidence of linguistic bias.

The Task Force will distribute the completed report to all 50 states and will act as a clearinghouse for information on eliminating sex bias from state codes.

Credit

Into the early 1970's access to credit and terms of credit policies discriminated against women based on sex and marital status. For example, women's loan applications had to be countersigned by additional persons, usually men; mortgages were almost unobtainable; and banks refused to consider the salary of wives, along with their husbands', in joint applications unless the wife could prove that she was not capable of bearing children.

Initially, state laws were enacted to prohibit these discriminatory practices. In 1968, Congress passed federal legislation aimed at prohibiting sex discrimination in consumer loan applications (i.e., the Truth in Lending, Fair Credit Billing, Fair Credit Reporting, and Consumer Leasing Acts).

More comprehensive federal legislation was enacted by Congress in 1978, prohibiting discrimination based on sex or marital status by financial institutions in all credit transactions: the Equal Credit Opportunity Act (ECOA) (15 U.S.C. section 1691, et. seq.).

The Act requires financial institutions to make credit equally available to all credit worthy customers without regard to sex or marital status, to inform unsuccessful applicants of the reasons for denial of their rights under the Act, and to retain pertinent documents. In 1976 ECOA was amended to extend its protections to discrimination based on age, religion, race and national origin.

The broad language of ECOA neither specifically includes business credit customers nor excludes them from the antidiscrimination protections. However, the federal regulation directing the implementation of ECOA, "Regulation B," 12 C.F.R. section 202 et. seq., does distinguish between consumer and business credit, 12 C.F.R. section 202 (e). Under Regulation B, business credit transactions are exempt from four important ECOA protections:

- creditors may inquire as to marital status

- notification of reasons for adverse action need not be supplied unless so requested within 30 days of oral or written notice of denial

- the business creditor may disregard regulations requiring furnishing credit information to consumer reporting agencies

- records need not be retained unless specifically requested in writing by an applicant within 90 days of the adverse action.

When the business exemptions were originally proposed, the Federal Reserve Board reflected a belief that applicants for business credit were more sophisticated and therefore more familiar with the credit process and less likely to need explanations of adverse credit actions (Federal Reserve Board press release of November 3, 1976 at p. 15 (Docket No. R-0031)). However, in October of 1978, responding to staff and public concern, the Board invited comment on a proposed rule that would have extended the ECOA requirements to business credit (43 Fed Reg 203 (Oct. 26, 1978) Reg B Docket No. R-0185).

Hundreds of comments were submitted to the Federal Reserve Board. The majority came from banks and lending institutions and were in opposition to the proposals. Substantially fewer comments were submitted by public interest groups (civil and women's rights), legal aid offices and government agencies. These comments generally supported the proposals.

Opponents stressed the physical and financial burdens the proposed protections of business credit transactions would pose to lending institutions. Business loans usually involve a greater volume of documents than do consumer loan applications; additional record-keeping and retention of documents would prove expensive and unwieldy. Notification is referred to as sound business practice but one which need not be required by statute. The prohibition on inquiring as to marital status was regarded as "inconsequential" in light of the close relationship existent between creditors and business applicants.

In contrast, proponents stressed the inherent discrimination of inquiring into sex and marital status of applicants for business loans, just as it has been so determined in the case of consumer loan applications. ECOA does permit inquiries regarding circumstances of ownership of all assets relied upon in extending credit--thus including any interest a spouse may have where relevant to the credit application (202.5(d)(1)). Therefore, the marital status of business applicants is even less likely to be relevant to credit applications than it is for consumer applications. Furthermore, proponents agreed that extending the notification of reasons for adverse action provision to small businesses (i.e., the proposal spoke of a $100,000 cutoff), would ensure the awareness of frequently inexperienced borrowers of their rights under ECOA. Considering the voluminous documentation involved in business loan applications, notification would require a minor additional effort by banks. However, this minor effort would secure the protection of important rights of the loan applicant. Proponents underscored the belief that aggrieved applicants must know how and where to address their complaints and to seek advice if ECOA is to serve as an effective mechanism for law enforcement.

Lastly, proponents emphasized that providing for the retention of relevant records would not entail the "burdensome" retention of all documents but it would ensure successful oversight of compliance with ECOA by lending institutions.

Effective October 15, 1982, the Federal Reserve Board withdrew the proposed rulemaking. The Board found that the inconvenience to banks outweighed the benefit to the rights of business applicants:

cost and burdens associated with the proposed amendments outweighed their possible benefits, which the Board judged to be slight in view of the basic requirements of the regulation. (Federal Reserve Board press release, October 14, 1982).

However, the Board noted that ECOA protections against discrimination do remain effective:

The proposed amendments related only to the mechanical requirements of the regulation, and their withdrawal does not affect the substantive provisions of the Equal Credit Opportunity Act and Regulation B, which continue to prohibit discrimination on the basis of sex, marital status, race, etc. in any aspect of a business credit transaction. (emphasis added; Federal Reserve Board press release, Oct 14, 1982).

A second issue regarding women's access to commercial credit arises as a result of the ECOA exemption to community property states from compliance with the marital status inquiries. Because ownership of marital property is shared equally between husband and wife in community property jurisdictions, the act permits inquiry, in those states, into an applicant's marital status.

While the law, on its face, appears to be justified, there is some criticism of its application. In effect, married men are not affected by the exemption while married women are subject to more scrupulous investigation and review and may be denied credit as a result thereof.

Numerous law review articles describe ECOA, Regulation B and related litigation, but few focus on the business or property exemptions or any other specific interests of women entrepreneurs. A mere handful of law review articles (and effectively no other publications) directly address legal issues regarding women's access to commercial credit. The articles are identified in this bibliography.

It appears that the actual comments submitted to the Federal Reserve Board concerning the proposed rulemaking provide much of the most pertinent information and analysis regarding access to business credit. Judging from these comments, the following offices and organizations have conducted substantial research and analysis in support of ECOA protection for women business owners:

Women's Legal Defense Fund, 2000 P St., N.W., Suite 40, Washington D.C. 20036;

National Organization for Women - National NOW Credit Committee.

U.S. Department of Justice: the Task Force on Sex Discrimination, the Civil Rights Division & the Housing & Credit Section, Washington, D.C.;

National Association of Women Business Owners, Chicago, IL.

Women's Equity Action League, 1250 Eye Street N.W., Suite 305, Washington, D.C. 20005; and of course

U.S. Small Business Administration, Office of Women's Business Ownership, Washington, D.C. 20416.

Citations

Blakely, Susan Smith. "Credit Opportunity for Women: The ECOA And Its Effects." Wisconsin L. Rev (1981): 655.

The primary focus of this article is on the evolution, applications and analysis of the "effects test" to sex-based ECOA challenges. However, the author does mention both Regulation B exemptions which are of importance to women business owners: the business exemptions and the community property exemption. Noting the legislative history of ECOA, the author reveals that while the Federal Reserve merely intended to protect consumer credit (with the promulgation of Regulation B), the legislature did not distinguish between business and consumer credit:

Such a distinction and the resulting exemption for business credit may be serious denials of protection to an increasing number of women who are active in the work force and the business world.

Dearhammer, William. "Equal Credit Opportunity Act/Regulation B - Application to Business Credit." The Journal of Commercial Bank Lending (September 1981): 2-12 .

This is an outline of the mechanics of ECOA and Regulation B as concerns business credit. The author does not question ECOA's applicability to business credit but rather explains the broad and direct implications of ECOA thereon.

A creditor may not discriminate on the prohibited bases--sex, race, color, religion, etc.; but, the author explains, these bases do not "easily" apply, or may be circumvented by banks in the case of business applicants. It is cautioned however, that any information used by a bank in assessing credit worthiness must have a "demonstrable relationship" to that determination. For example, judging persons without briefcases to be poor risks, unworthy of credit extentions, would be prohibited under Regulation B "since the policy would tend to lead to adverse action against women more often than against men."

Notice and record retention requirements are also explained. The author concludes with recommendations to lending institutions for staying abreast of ECOA and suggests preventive measures to assure bank compliance with Regulation B.

O'Connor, William J. Jr. "The Equal Credit Opportunity Act and Business Credit--Some Problems Considered." The Journal of Commercial Bank Lending (January 1979): 20-36.

The article addresses several "troublesome" provisions of Regulation B in an effort to "dispel the confusion" of lenders surrounding the Regulation.

Initally lenders assumed ECOA to be merely a consumer credit statute; they were surprised by its application to business credit as a consequence of the adoption of Regulation B. The legislative developments are described (including the 1976 amendments, congressional restraints on the limitation of ECOA's applicability, and the ECOA exemptions).

The ECOA business exemptions are individually described and commented upon:

● The marital status exemption--The author states that this exemption, "seems to be a correct and sensible approach," in that this information normally would be known by the creditor. The proposed repeal of this exemption, because it dilutes ECOA protections, is not considered a significant matter.

● The notification exemption--The author criticizes the language of the exemption for failing to clearly state the obligations and time constraints it imposes upon banks.

● The furnishing credit information exemption--The author cautions that confusion exists because consumer loans are sometimes made in the commercial department of banks. Banks must take care to limit the exemption to business loans.

● The record retention exemption--Conflicting provisions of Regulation B imply that in order for a bank to ensure compliance it should keep all business credit documents for at least 120 days.

Other issues addressed include: problems surrounding the effects test doctrine, the definition of an "application" and the need for standardized procedures. Additionally, the question of when co-signers may be required is an important consideration for women business owners. ECOA prohibits a bank from requiring "the signature of the applicant's spouse or other person" on an application where the applicant is credit worthy. However, this provision only applies to limited extents in community property and other jurisdictions depending on whether spouses may make property available for the other spouses' indebtedness. Again, the author is critical of the vagueness and incongruencies of Regulation B provisions.

Center for Women Policy Studies. Women and Credit: An Annotated Bibliography. Washington, D.C.: 1974). Out of Print.

A pre-ECOA publication which is useful in locating materials describing the historical context in which ECOA was drafted. The brief annotations cover the following types of reference materials: newspaper, newsletter and magazine articles; special credit reports and surveys; government regulations; legal documents; statements and testimony; published research; unpublished papers; and materials on labor force earnings and job turnover.

Section III: Annotated Bibliography

Characteristics of Women Business Owners

Published Books and Articles

Beattie, L. Elisabeth. "The Entrepreneurial Woman." Business and Economic Review 31,1 (October 1984): 3-6.

This article discusses similarities and differences between male and female entrepreneurs. Both feel the need to achieve and be independent, and both tend to start businesses out of economic necessity. However, although the number of women-owned businesses is growing faster than the number of businesses owned by men, women's businesses lag behind in productivity and earning power.

Becker, Eugene H. "Self-employed Workers: An Update to 1983." Monthly Labor Review 107, 7 (July 1984): 14-18.

This article focuses on trends in self-employment since 1979. In 1983 nonagricultural self-employment was 7.6 million (an increase of 45 percent over 1970). The category "self-employed" includes those whose primary job involves working for themselves in their own business, profession, trade or farm. Individuals who work for a corporation of which they are the major owners are counted as wage and salary workers (such individuals numbered 2.8 million in 1982). Wage and salary workers who are self-employed in their secondary job are also excluded (1.6 million people in 1980).

According to the figures presented in this article, women were only 29 percent of the self-employed in 1983, while they comprised 45 percent of wage and salary workers. However, the number of self-employed women is increasing five times faster than the number of self-employed men. Women are entering self-employment at a faster rate than their overall entry into the labor force, indicating that they are trying to create employment opportunities for themselves. Both women and men who are self-employed earn less than their wage and salary counterparts, and self-employed women earn considerably less then self-employed men. In 1982 the median level of earnings of self-employed women was $6,644, as compared with $14,360 for men. This discrepancy can be partially explained by the fact that more than half of self-employed women are in relatively low-paying sales and service occupations, while about one-third of self-employed men are in higher paying management, professional, finance and business sales occupations.

Bender, Henry. <u>Report on Women Business Owners</u>. New York: American Management Association, June 1, 1978.

A survey of successful women business owners was conducted by the American Management Association (AMA) concurrently with the survey of the President's Task Force on Women Business Owners. The results of this survey were published as an appendix to President's Task Force Report, <u>The Bottom Line: Unequal Enterprise in America</u>.

Based on the responses of a sample of 264 women business owners, the AMA reported on personal and demographic characteristics of successful women business owners, characteristics of their businesses, the owners' backgrounds, perceived business-related problems and general feelings about owning a business. As did Schreier and Schwartz, they concluded that male and female entrepreneurs are very much alike, but that the women may face greater obstacles to business ownership, especially in acquiring adequate initial financing.

The AMA profile of the successful woman business owner showed that she:

- came from a close, supportive family

- was married to a supportive husband who was either a business owner or a professional

- exhibited strong entrepreneurial drive early in life

- tended to be highly educated

- exhibited inordinate capacity for hard work and dedication to her enterprise

- was well informed concerning her business field

- had ability to juggle and integrate diverse aspects of her life, including roles of family life and

- had ability to redirect negative situations and attitudes to her advantage.

Most of the women (52.4 percent) started their businesses alone and over half owned retail and service businesses. Their businesses became profitable quite soon (34.5 percent within one year and another 28.1 percent within three years)--a success the AMA called "remarkable." Despite this success, and the fact that about one-third of those surveyed had gross receipts of one-quarter million dollars or more, most provided their own initial financing from personal savings. This illustrates how critically important the problem of initial financing is to the woman business owner.

Bettner, Gill and Christine Donahue. "Now They're Not Laughing." Forbes
132, 12 (November 21, 1983): 116-130.

This article touches on the generalities of the female entrepreneur's experience, as well as profiling nine individual women business owners. One expert
interviewed for the article argues that women start their own businesses to
generate income, rather than wealth, and are more often satisfied with moder-
ate as opposed to remarkable success. However, the women business owners who
were interviewed revealed a wide variety of reasons for creating their own
ventures, and they tended to be very successful financially.

Bird, Caroline. Enterprising Women. New York: Norton, 1976.

A Bicentennial project of the Business and Professional Women's Foundation,
this book is a collection of short biographies of successful women in U.S.
history. Many of the women profiled were entrepreneurs. The book helps to
show that American women have been involved in business ownership and the
professions since Independence, and highlights their abilities and achieve-
ments. Includes a bibliography and an index.

Buerk, Susan C. "Women's Opportunity: Starting Your Own Business." Vital Speeches 44 (February 1, 1978): 230-232.

The author argues that women have special hurdles to overcome in any business
relationship. At the time this was written, available data indicated that
women owned fewer than 5 percent of all U.S. businesses and only 11,000 women
owners earned more than $25,000 per year. The author argues that conscious
or unconscious attitudes held by men and women constitute barriers to women's
business ownership. These attitudes include: social--men seeing women as
primarily "helpers"; sexual--a negative element involving the male ego; and
intellectual--women simply having less business experience than men. The
author points out that women have stereotypes about themselves in business.
She feels women tend to be passive; doubt and underestimate themselves; and
need to develop self-confidence.

Burr, Pat A. "A Look at the Female Entrepreneur." American Journal of
Small Business 2 (January 1978): 1-4.

In this guest editorial by the former Assistant Administrator for Management
Assistance of the U.S. Small Business Administration, the 1972 census data on
women-owned businesses are reviewed and attention drawn to the small number
of women-owned, and especially, minority women-owned firms.

Business and Professional Women's Foundation. Profile of Business and Professional Women. Washington, D.C.: National Federation of Business and Professional Women's Clubs, 1970.

The 1970 Profile presents an analysis and interpretation of the results of a 1969 survey of the members of the National Federation of Business and Professional Women's Clubs. It also provides some comparisons with corresponding national figures for all males and all females. Categories such as the following are examined: occupation, income, type of employment, education, age, marital status, dependents, residence, political activities, social status, and membership in the BPW clubs and other organizations. Approximately 19.1 percent of BPW members responding to the survey were self-employed.

Campbell, Bebe Moore. "These Women Mean Business." Black Enterprise 14, 11 (June 1984): 224-228.

This article profiles Sharon Poindexter and Marilyn French Hubbard. Ms. Poindexter, the first black president of the National Association of Women Business Owners (NAWBO) and President of Poindexter Associates, a management consulting firm in Kansas City, believes that women-owned businesses fail because women need more practical business skills. Ms. Hubbard is president and founder of the National Association of Black Women Enterpreneurs and the owner of Marilyn Hubbard Associates in Detroit, Michigan.

Carsrud, Alan L. and Kenneth W. Olm. "The Success of Male & Female Entrepreneurs: A Comparative Analysis of the Effects of Multi-Dimensional Achievement Motivation and Personality Traits." Innovation in Business ed. Smilor and Kuhn. New York: Praeger, 1985.

This article explores the interaction of the motivation and personalities of male and female business owners. The samples include present and potential owners. There were two studies conducted, one of 103 male owners of retail building supply firms with gross sales over $500,000 annually and between 4 and 55 employees. Ninety-six individuals responded. The second study, of women entrepreneurs, utilized a sample of 246 women in the Austin, TX area who owned more than 50 percent equity in their businesses and had gross annual revenues of under $1 million. Of the sample, 108 women responded. The article does not specify if the same instrument was utilized in both surveys. Unlike the male sample, the women's businesses were representative of a "wide variety of industrial categories."

Carsrud, Alan L., K.W. Olm and Ross D. Ahlgren. "Some Observations on Female Entrepreneurs and Female MBA Students: Initiating a Five-Year Study." Working Paper #84/85-4-32. Austin, TX: Graduate School of Business, University of Texas at Austin, 1984.

This paper compares the psychological and motivational profiles of women recent MBA graduates with successful women entrepreneurs. Significant differences were found between the two groups in: interpersonal competitiveness, mastery needs, verbal aggressiveness and hostility characteristics. Comments are included on graduate programs of business in terms of the effect of these programs' climate and educational paradigms on graduates entering entrepreneurial ventures. Tests administered in this preliminary study include: Work and Family Orientation Inventory (WOFO), a multi-dimensional scale, and the Extended Personality Attributes Questionnaire (EPAQ). Results were analyzed using a multi-variate analysis of variance with the two groups of subjects and the eight scales of the achievement motivation and personality measures as the independent variables. Findings showed: women MBA students were more interpersonally competitive, and higher in mastery scores, as well as more verbally aggressive and hostile than women entrepreneurs.

The authors conclude that the women MBA graduates show high incidence of maladaptive traits since they claim verbal aggressiveness, hostility and extreme competition have been consistently found to be not adaptive to business success in male and female entrepreneurs. The article raises questions about business school admission processes as well as educational program structure in the light of these findings and calls for definitive research into specific business school course content and effectiveness in promoting entrepreneurism. Bibliography included.

Carsrud, Alan L., K.W. Olm and G. Eddy. "Entrepreneurship: Research in Quest of a Paradigm." The Art and Science of Entrepreneurship ed. Sexton and Smilor. Cambridge, MA: Ballinger, 1985.

This article describes a research model for studying entrepreneurship which is used by the Research Group on Entrepreneurship at the University of Texas at Austin. Four "primary causal" factors are being studied (psychological, personal/demographic, organizational/sociological and situational/environmental) and two "secondary predictor variables" (current business stage and type of business operation and industrial sector). Gender is one of the "primary causal" variables now under scrutiny. The article also critiques the work of some commentators who group "entrepreneurs into broad, over-generalized classifications such as 'female entrepreneurs' without regard to the specific businesses and economic sector they have chosen (and why)... [which] only increases the imprecision of the research results and interpretations generated."

Charlboneau, F. Jill. "The Woman Entrepreneur." American Demographics
   (June 1981): 21-23.

The author reviews the findings of the 1977 Census of Women-Owned Businesses which reported that over 5,000 female-owned firms had receipts of over $1 million and that the typical woman entrepreneur is unmarried, white, college-educated, and about 52 years of age. The number of women entrepreneurs in the United States has more than doubled since 1972, and Charlboneau estimates that there are about one million of them today. California has more businesses owned by women than any other state, with one-third in Los Angeles. Nearly half of womens' businesses are concentrated in services, with 30 percent in retailing.

According to the author, the greatest obstacle for women entrepreneurs is dealing with the banking and financial community which is overwhelming male. She agrees with many authors who feel that women lack confidence and do not understand money, but points out that there are organizations that specialize in training women entrepreneurs. The article cites the Small Business Administration training programs for women as well as the American Woman's Economic Development Corporation in New York City as examples.

   Cook, Jane T. and Jane Widerman. "Women: The Best Entrepreneurs."
      Canadian Business 55, 6 (June 1982): 68-73.

This article outlines the results of a survey of sole proprietorships in the United States and Canada conducted by Thorne Riddell in 1970 and 1980. The study concluded that the proportion of new women-owned businesses that were still in operation three years after their founding was twice that of new businesses owned or managed by men. The successful businesses were those whose owners had done extensive research prior to starting the venture, had sought professional assistance and had received business training.

   The authors of the article assert that women's ability to bring their businesses through a period of economic slowdown more successfully than men foreshadows their future dominance of new business start-ups. They argue that within three years women might even be running the majority of the estimated 60,000 new businesses started in Canada in 1982.

   Cuba, Richard, David DeCenzo, and Andrea Annish. "Management Practices
      of Successful Female Business Owners." American Journal of Small Busi-
      ness 8, 2 (October - December, 1983): 40-46.

This study is based on a survey of 58 women business owners in Atlanta, Baltimore and Richmond. The women in the sample were identified through telephone directories, but the authors do not disclose what percentage of women business owners identified by this method did not respond to the survey. Most of the businesses were in retail trade; a few were in services. Over half were five years old or less, and nearly 75 percent had annual sales under $125,000.

Spearman rank correlations and chi-square tests were used to test which characteristics contribute to business success among women business owners. The authors found that the financial success of women business owners was associated with delegation of key tasks to employees, higher levels of education and more prior work experience.

DeCarlo, J.F. and P.R. Lyons. "A Comparison of Selected Personal Characteristics of Minority and Non-Minority Female Entrepreneurs." Journal of Small Business Management 17 (October 1979): 22-29.

In this study DeCarlo and Lyons attempt to apply to female entrepreneurs the EPPS (Edwards Personal Preference Schedule) and the SIV (Gordon Survey of Interpersonal Values) tests, that were used by Hornaday and Aboud in studying male entrepreneurs. The standardized tests were used to evaluate differences between minority and non-minority female entrepreneurs, and between female entrepreneurs and the general population.

The sample for this study was drawn from the business and manufacturing directories of several mid-Atlantic states. Out of a sample of 122 women-owned businesses, 45 were owned by minority women. Most were concentrated in the retail and service sectors--81.6 percent of non-minority and 83.7 percent of minority firms.

The results showed that the minority women were somewhat older, started their businesses later in life, had more involvement with previous enterpreneurial efforts, were more likely to have been married, had less education, were more willing to accept regimentation, and were more likely to have started their businesses alone than the non-minority women.

In general, the entrepreneurs placed higher on the achievement, aggression, autonomy, independence, and leadership scales, but lower on support, conformity, and benevolence than the female population as a whole, as measured by the EPPS and SIV tests. Non-minority female entrepreneurs put higher value on achievement, support, recognition, and independence, while minorities placed higher value on conformity and benevolence.

_____. "The Emerging Female Entrepreneur: Who Is She?" Proceedings, Annual Meeting of the Academy of Management. Atlanta (1979).

In what appears to be a preliminary assessment or background study supporting their later work, DeCarlo and Lyons describe the characteristics of a sample of 122 women business owners (drawn from a population of 783 that were listed in business directories in the mid-Atlantic region). It was found that the women in the sample generally exhibited characteristics similar to those of all women business owners (as measured by the 1972 census).

Results showed that for the sample the average number of employees was 7.3 persons; 53 percent had less than five employees. The women reported an average length of experience of 6.5 years in their current type of business and 9.2 years in some other line of business. The average age of their present business was 5.5 years. Only 9.1 percent took over an already existing business, and 52 percent started their businesses alone.

The median age of the women was 39 years, and 88 percent had been married (42 percent divorced or separated). Medium to high parental expectations were reported by 86 percent of the women. Most (40 percent) described themselves as having been an independent child. They demonstrated little willingness to accept regimentation and reported they had high energy levels. Of the sample, 59 percent graduated from college, and 46 percent reported that there were other self-employed members in their immediate families.

DeCarlo and Lyons point out that the women surveyed tended to be younger than their male counterparts and to work fewer hours. But after mentioning these differences the authors concluded that overall "there is similarity between male and female entrepreneurs on descriptive characteristics." Not discussed, however, were possible differences in the distribution of male and female-owned businesses among the industries and differences in receipts, two differences that are cited by other observers.

Devine, Marion and David Clutterbuck. "The Rise of the Entrepreneuse."
Management Today (January 1985): 62-65, 105-107.

The authors argue that British women get around the barriers of a male-dominated business world by becoming entrepreneurs, or "entrepreneuses". The authors contend that these British "entrepreneuses" are generally less visible than their American counterparts. British women starting their own businesses are looking for: (1) a way to work outside of stereotypical female jobs (2) a way to be creative and (3) a way to develop specific job skills. The article argues, in conclusion, that as the "entrepreneuse" phenomenon grows, so will the need for government assistance.

Eliason, Carol. Entrepreneurship for Women: An Unfilled Agenda. Columbus, OH: Ohio State University, National Center for Research on Vocational Education, 1981.

This paper outlines characteristics and needs of women small business owners and discusses recent developments in entrepreneurship education. The focus is on vocational guidance and education. The author describes educational materials for entrepreneurship, government programs for women entrepreneurs, and private sector initiatives in entrepreneurship training for women.

"The Entrepreneur Sees Herself as Manager." Harvard Business Review (July-August, 1982).

An interview with Lore Harp who started Vector Graphics, a microcomputer firm, provided the basis for this article. The firm went public in 1981 and Ms. Harp is the Chief Executive Officer. In the interview she discusses her background; her dissatisfaction with the role of housewife; the beginnings of

Vector, and how she and a friend/partner nurtured it; the rapid growth of the firm; and the attention to marketing, services, and support that distinguished Vector from other microcomputer companies.

"Entrepreneurial Eighties." American Demographics 7, 1 (January 1985): 11.

This brief article reports on the results of a Department of Labor study of self-employed workers in the United States (See Becker, above). The study found that a long-term decline in self-employment began to reverse itself in the 1970's. During the 1980's, the growth of non-farm self-employment has averaged 2.7 percent per year, while wage and salary employment has grown by only 0.4 percent per year. During that time the increase in numbers of self-employed women has been five times greater than the increase in numbers of self-employed men, and three times greater than the increase in the number of female wage and salary workers.

Finney, Ruth S. Towards a Typology of Women Entrepreneurs: Their Business Ventures and Family Life. Honolulu, Hawaii: East-West Center, 1977.

This paper presents preliminary data from a longitudinal study, "Project Womanstart," at the East-West Center in Hawaii. It uses a case study approach based on interviews with 50 women business owners.

The major differences found among the women entrepreneurs were attributed to the types of businesses they entered--"female" businesses, those that involved products or services typically associated with women, or "masculine" businesses. Finney's findings suggest that the women who owned "feminine" businesses had their businesses at home more often, were younger, had younger children when they started their businesses, experienced less discrimination, and had lower levels of gross revenues than those women with "masculine" businesses. The owners of "masculine" businesses reported they were discriminated against when applying for credit and were treated poorly by salespeople and employees.

This distinction between "masculine" and "feminine" businesses, which is analogous to the traditional/non-traditional distinction used in studies of occupational segregation in the labor market seems to be a useful one. It highlights the fact that women-owned businesses are concentrated in low-growth, lowreceipts industries, especially those which provide services and retail outlets for other women. There are very few women-owned businesses in the dynamic "masculine" industries where expansion is more likely. However, this issue is only hinted at in Finney's work, and then only at the beginning of the paper.

Overall, the women surveyed most frequently gave the following reasons for going into business:

● had a good idea and wanted to create something with it

- wanted to give a needed service or product to others

- knew they would be good at it

- wanted to set own hours and place of work

- wanted to supplement the family income

- got tired of working at a dead-end job for someone else.

The author argues that for women, creativity or helping others may be alternatives to competition as an entry point or motivator to entrepreneurship. The women interviewed seemed to want approval, appreciation, and recognition that what they were doing was appropriate for women. Finney questions whether the "stereotype of the entrepreneur fits the stereotype of the 'normal, healthy woman' which many women have internalized," suggests that the process of women's socialization may be a barrier to entrepreneurship.

Gillis, Phyllis. Entrepreneurial Mothers. New York: Rawson Associates, 1983.

The author argues that many women enter business ownership because they find it difficult to balance the demands of working for someone else with household and family responsibilities. Statistics showing more rapid increases in self-employment for women than for men are explained by the rising trends in women's labor force participation combined with the current "baby boomlet."

The book, which contains anecdotal information on balancing child care and business ownership as well as practical advice for mothers who want to start their own businesses, is based on over 200 interviews with mothers who are business owners. It suggests nine very small or "micro" businesses that offer good opportunities for combining motherhood and work: health and beauty businesses, food and entertaining, computer businesses, crafts, construction and home improvement, sales, social services, community-based businesses, and child-based businesses.

Goffee, Robert and Richard Scase. "Business Ownership and Women's Subordination: A Preliminary Study of Female Proprietors." Sociological Review (London) 31, 4 (November 1983): 625-644.

The article presents an analysis of women's business ownership from a Marxist perspective. It draws on unstructured interviews with a non-random sample of 23 women business owners in Great Britain to determine women's reasons for entering business ownership, and whether business ownership has furthered women's emancipation and self-determination.

In Great Britain, while women are 40 percent of the total labor force, they are only 20 percent of the self-employed. Eighty percent of women-owned businesses are in the service sector.

The women interviewed started their own businesses mainly because they had difficulty finding wage and salary work, they wanted to be their own boss, or they wanted to enter a field that was difficult for women to break into. The authors argue that although business proprietorship offers women the potential of financial independence, in fact women become dependent on men for finance, technical and professional services, and their domestic work responsibilities often increase. However, they conclude that business ownership contributes to a development of feminist consciousness.

_____. Women in Charge: The Experiences of Women Entrepreneurs. London: George Allen and Unwin., 1984.

Grayson, Paul E., Janet Barnhardt and Sandra Byberg. "Male and Female Operated Nonfarm Proprietorships, Tax Year 1980." SOI Bulletin. (U.S. Department of Treasury, Internal Revenue Service, Spring, 1983).

According to this article, produced by the IRS Research Division, male sole proprietors earned ten times as much as female sole proprietors in Tax Year 1980; and female proprietors were slightly more likely (63 percent) to have their businesses at home than men (60 percent). Men who operated their businesses outside the home had business receipts three times higher than their female counterparts. The article contains extensive tables.

Gregg, Gail. "Women Entrepreneurs: The Second Generation." Across the Board 22, 1 (January 1985): 10-18.

The author argues that a new generation of female entrepreneurs has emerged which has more in common with male entrepreneurs than did their predecessors. Although they still cite discrimination, social pressures, and lack of confidence, women entrepreneurs today are more independent, aggressive, creative and frustrated when they are not in charge--traits common to their male counterparts.

The article summarizes the results of the Hisrich and Brush study (see below) of 468 women entrepreneurs, most of whom were operators of small retail and service businesses--bakeries, boutiques, and decorating firms--typical of "first generation" women entrepreneurs.

According to the author, the second generation is that of the young urban professional woman entrepreneur, who has business training or special technical skills. A woman from the new generation is "more likely to start her own company with the help of professional contacts, financial savvy, a sophisticated business plan, and a heightened desire to make money, rather than simply wanting to 'do something'." The article includes several interviews with women business owners of the "second generation."

Gumpert, David. "The Gender Factor." <u>Working Woman</u> (September 1983): 162, 164.

The author reviews the studies of women business owners by Welsch and Young and Hisrich and Brush which have identified the following differences between male and female business owners:

- women research business ideas more carefully

- women are more realistic about economic conditions

- women are less technically/scientifically oriented

- women start fewer innovative businesses than men

- women have more trouble with financial management

The article also lists the similarities between men and women business owners reported in these two studies, in personal characteristics and family background.

Halcomb, R. <u>Women Making It: Patterns and Profiles of Success</u>. New York: Atheneum, 1979.

This book profiles successful women from many different fields, and discusses a variety of issues related to women achieving success, i.e., career analysis, investments, networking/mentoring, and family. One chapter focuses on interviews with five women business owners, most of whom started their businesses because they had trouble advancing in the companies where they worked. The author reports that many of these women found that "instead of coping with the sexism of bosses, one copes with the same attitude in clients and customers."

Hisrich, Robert D. "The Woman Entrepreneur in Puerto Rico." In The Factors of Entrepreneurship: The Experience in Puerto Rico. 1982.

The purpose of this study is to determine if women entrepreneurs in Puerto Rico exhibit the same demographic backgrounds, personality traits, attitudes and business problems as the U.S. "mainland" women studied in earlier work by the author (Hisrich and Brush). The findings discussed in this paper are based on personal interviews with 15 women entrepreneurs and 25 responses to a confidential questionnaire mailed to 72 women entrepreneurs in Puerto Rico. The survey instrument used was similar to the one designed for the Hisrich and Brush national survey.

The author found that the Puerto Rican women entrepreneurs surveyed come from well-educated, financially secure, middle to upper class backgrounds. Their businesses were located in Puerto Rico. While operating diverse businesses, almost all are in traditional "women's" fields. The only problems identified by the women entrepreneurs related to being women were in obtaining financing. The women's self-assessments of their business skills, motivations, and business problems are discussed in detail.

> _____. "The Woman Entrepreneur in the United States and Puerto Rico: A Comparative Study." Leadership and Organization Development Journal 5,5 (1984): 3-9.

This article summarizes a study of 468 female entrepreneurs from the United States, and 30 from Puerto Rico. Ninety percent of the Americans and 73 percent of the Puerto Ricans classified their businesses as service related. Both groups rated themselves highest in people management and lowest in financial management. Overall, the average female entrepreneur in both areas is 35 years old, married to a self-employed man and has a B.A. in liberal arts. Tables, references included.

> _____. "The Woman Entrepreneur: Minding Her Own Business." University of Tulsa Annual (1984-85): 52-58.

This article is an informal treatment of the issues raised in the author's academic research on women business owners. Quotations from successful women entrepreneurs around the country illustrate the barriers and motivators Hisrich and his colleagues identified in a nationwide study of over 1000 women business owners (see "The Woman Entrepreneur," Journal of Small Business Management, 1984).

> _____. "The Woman Entrepreneur: Characteristics, Skills, Problems and Prescriptions for Success." In The Encyclopedia of Entrepreneurship. New York: Ballinger Publishing Co., 1986.

This article reviews statistics on women business owners from standard data sources. The author claims there are significant differences between the motivation, business skill levels and occupational backgrounds of women and men entrepreneurs. References for this article include the study by Smith, McCain and Warren which also claims significant differences among business owners by gender. (See: "Women Entrepreneurs Really Are Different," Proceedings, 1982 Conference on Entrepreneurship, June, 1982).

> Hisrich, Robert D. and Donald D. Bowen. "The Female Entrepreneur: A Career Development Perspective." Academy of Management Review (April 1986).

The author states the thesis of this article as follows: "... means must be found to desegregate the entrepreneurial ghettoes of women in the retail and service trades. The research proposed here offers a new approach --- a careers perspective ... to better develop ... female entrepreneurs ... in nontraditional industries."

This article utilizes a conceptual model of a "life-cycle approach to career research" developed by Sonnenfeld and Kotter ("The Maturation of Career Theory," Human Relations 35, 1982: 19-46) to categorize "recent research on entrepreneurial careers... and to identify gaps in available knowledge." The author concludes that since "there have not been any studies of adult development history for female entrepreneurs...[and] given the centrality of adult development in contemporary career theory... this presents a serious problem for development of a theory of female entrepreneurs' careers." The author suggests "a valuable preliminary step [would use] the intensive life history approach applied by Levinson (1978)... [including] a combination of psychometric tests and intensive interviewing..." A table is included which catalogs the author's conclusions about important issues to be addressed in future research, and a list of references including studies from various fields which may shed light on research needed on career patterns of women business owners.

Hisrich, Robert D. and Candida Brush. "The Woman Entrepreneur: Implications of Family, Educational and Occupational Experience." Frontiers of Entrepreneurship Research: Proceedings, 1983 Conference on Entrepreneurship (Babson College, 1983): 255-270.

This article describes in some detail the findings of the authors' survey of 468 women business owners (see entry below) "in terms of the demographic composition of the sample, the entrepreneurial venture, and the management skills of the entrepreneurs." Eleven tables are included, including 7 on demographics. Tables of particular interest are those on self appraisal of management skill (nearly half saw themselves as fair to poor in financial matters); reasons for becoming involved in entrepreneurship (nearly half did so "out of job frustration"); gross business revenues in 1981 (nearly half had gross revenues under $100,000); employees (72% had 0-4 employees; and 66% employed no family members).

_____. "The Woman Entrepreneur: Management Skills and Business Problems." Journal of Small Business Management 22, 1 (January 1984): 30-37.

This article summarizes the results of the authors' survey of 468 women business owners from 18 states. Questionnaires were sent to a random sample of 1,151 women business owners who had been selected from mailing lists of trade associations and state agencies. Of those who responded, 55 percent were married and had children and 68 percent had attended college or graduate school. Over half were the first born in their families, and the majority had fathers who had been self-employed.

The respondents' businesses tended to be small; 72 percent had four employees or less, and 30 percent had no employees. The form of ownership varied a great deal--43 percent of the businesses were corporations, 35 percent sole proprietorships and 12 percent partnerships. Ninety percent of the businesses were in sales and services; only 7 percent were in manufacturing, and

3 percent in finance. The women cited lack of business and financial training, obtaining credit, and lack of collateral as their biggest business problems.

The article concludes with recommendations on how to promote and assist women's business ownership. Tables are provided.

_____. "Women and Minority Entrepreneurs: A Comparative Analysis." Frontiers of Entrepreneurship Research: Proceedings, 1985 Conference on Entrepreneurship (Babson College, 1985).

This article reviews previous research on both women (minority and non-minority) and minority (male and female) entrepreneurs and describes findings from a survey of respondents to a questionnaire mailed to 1,000 randomly selected minority business owners listed in an unspecified "government publication." These findings were compared to those from an earlier study of women business owners by the authors (see entry on Hisrich and Brush, 1983). Major differences between the two groups are reported, including: nature of business venture, self-appraisal of personality and business skill, and (somewhat less defined) types of business problems faced.

Hisrich, Robert D. and Marie O'Brien. "The Woman Entrepreneur as a Reflection of the Type of Business." Frontiers of Entrepreneurship Research: Proceedings, 1982 Conference on Entrepreneurship. (Babson College, 1982): 54-67

The authors report findings similar to those outlined in their earlier paper (see below), using the same sample of women business owners. The results of this study indicate that women entrepreneurs exhibit some different characteristics than their male counterparts. They are more educated and older than both the general populace and male entrepreneurs, as measured by previous studies.

The women surveyed had very supportive parents and husbands. They exhibited strong entrepreneurial drive early in their lives which they attributed to the influence of both parents, although they appeared to have a stronger bond to the father. Female entrepreneurs in non-traditional business areas (finance, insurance, manufacturing and construction) differed from their counterparts in more "female traditional" business areas (retail and wholesale trade). Of particular importance is the apparent lack of external financing sources available in non-traditional business areas.

_____. "The Woman Entrepreneur from a Business and Sociological Perspective." Frontiers of Entrepreneurship Research: Proceedings, 1981 Conference on Entrepreneurship. (Babson College, 1982): 21-39.

The paper reports the results of a study of 21 female entrepreneurs in Massachusetts. The subjects were self-employed in various categories, more heavily weighted toward businesses that are non-traditional for females (including manufacturing, construction, computers, architectural and planning businesses).

Most of the women had been previously employed in professional fields, were married and were oldest in their families. They differed widely in age and education (although the educational level tended to be higher than average for women). A large percentage had self-employed fathers--this was particularly true for those in non-traditional fields. The most important motivations for starting their businesses were job satisfaction, independence and achievement. The women surveyed exhibited a strong correlation between desire to be an entrepreneur and achievement need. The biggest problems reported were financial, but marketing, management, and inventory control problems were also mentioned.

The authors concluded: "The results of this study suggest that female entrepreneurs experience varying business problems which more directly reflect the type of business than any educational or background characteristic of the respondent. Female entrepreneurs in non-traditional business areas (i.e., construction, manufacturing, computer services, and architecture and planning) experienced more significant problems than those in traditional ones, particularly in the areas of obtaining lines of credit, weak collateral position, and overcoming some of society's belief that women are not as serious as men about business."

Humphreys, Marie Adele and Jacquetta McClung. "Women Entrepreneurs in Oklahoma." Review of Regional Economics and Business 6 (October 1981) 13-20.

This study was conducted using a sample drawn from the 1979 Oklahoma Directory of Women in Business and Professions. From 176 questionnaires mailed, 86 usable responses were obtained. The findings of the Oklahoma survey were compared with the 1977 census findings. Most results were more or less comparable, but the Oklahoma women surveyed tended to have higher gross receipts than the national average.

The women entrepreneurs surveyed placed great importance on feelings of personal achievement and being one's own boss as components of job satisfaction, and found support from others less important. These findings were similar to those obtained by Hornaday and Aboud in their study of male entrepreneurs. The women believed hard work and personal determination, as well as management and financial acumen, were the keys to business success. This was also consistent with studies of male entrepreneurs.

The women listed the problems/obstacles they encountered in descending order of importance as follows:

● lack of previous business experience

● difficulty obtaining capital

● discrimination

- difficulty obtaining expert advice

- childraising responsibilities

- lack of self-confidence

- lack of encouragement from family and/or friends.

In comparing their findings to those of earlier studies of men, the authors point out that the major difference between men and women entrepreneurs was that the women had been successful employees before entering entrepreneurship. The authors suggested that these women entered entrepreneurship because of the lack of opportunities for advancement elsewhere. Women in the Oklahoma study (as well as in the Census) also tended to be more educated than men and more educated than women in general. This finding was considered important because male entrepreneurs usually have less education than the male population as a whole.

Hunt, S.D. "Women and Franchising." MSU Business Topics 26 (Spring 1978): 25-28.

Franchising accounts for one-third of retail sales and is growing rapidly. This study is based on a sample of 80 franchisors (those who grant franchises) drawn from listings in the Franchise Opportunities Handbook. They include franchisors in automotive service, convenience grocery/specialty stores, restaurants, business aids (i.e. tax and bookkeeping services), and employment services/agencies.

The results showed that women owned 6.5 percent of franchised businesses in 1976 and that 30.9 percent of franchised businesses were owned and managed by wife-husband teams.

In franchising, there is a trend toward company-owned and operated units, but the percentages of those managed by women is increasing (up to 14.2 percent in 1976 as compared with 11.4 percent in 1971). Involvement of women in franchising varies across industries. The greatest involvement of women is in employment services and convenience grocery/specialty shops; least in automotive services.

Most franchisors surveyed believed there was no difference in the general management performance of women as compared to men. Women were said to be better at customer relations and personal selling, but apparently had problems with the technical aspects of business operation, such as accounting, and with employee relations.

Leff, Laurel. "Franchise Fever." Working Woman (July 1983): 75-78.

The article refers to a survey by Shelby Hunt of Texas Tech University, which reports that 6.5 percent of all franchises are owned by women, and a further 31 percent are owned jointly by a husband and wife. The author contends that women are entering franchising at an increasing rate, although generally in the smaller businesses. One reason for this is the lower initial investment required for starting up certain franchises.

In addition to the background information summarized above, the article includes practical advice for prospective franchisees (franchise operators).

Lundborg, Louis B. "Survival of Women-Owned Businesses." Industry Week 207 (October 27, 1980): 136.

A short article appearing in the author's regular column, "Executive Survival Kit," reviews some unnamed studies on women-owned businesses, which he claims reveal that women have the same problems as do men with business ownership—especially in financial and personnel management.

McNamara, Patricia P. "Women Business Owners: Some Policy Issues and Questions from an Observer's Perspective." In The Regional Environments for Small Business and Entrepreneurship. Washington, D.C.: U.S. Small Business Administration, 1979.

This paper reviews government-generated publications and legislative actions related to women business owners. It traces the development of women's business enterprise policy prior to and during the Carter Administration.

The author also makes recommendations for government initiatives to help women move into a stronger economic position in business ownership. The main points discussed concern: data needs; evaluation of the ability of government programs (especially those of the Small Business Administration) to meet the needs of women business owners; access to capital for women business owners; and education, including management and technical assistance for women business owners.

Finally, the report reviews the findings of the 1972 Census of Women-Owned Businesses, paying particular attention to women-owned firms in Regional IX. It was found that in move industries the average Region IX woman-owned firm was larger than the average, woman-owned firm nationally, both in terms of number of employees per firm and average receipts per firm. The distribution of women-owned businesses among industries in Region IX was similar to the United States as a whole. It was also found that 86 percent of all Region IX women-owned firms were located in California.

McNamara, Patricia P. and Barbara McCaslin. The Women Entrepreneurs Project: Final Report. Los Angeles: University of California/Los Angeles, 1978.

The Women Entrepreneurs Project was a one-year project based at UCLA and funded by the U.S. Office of Education's Division of Vocational Education. As part of the project a questionnaire was sent to 532 women business owners in California. Results reported here were based on the answers of the 308 respondents.

The women's most frequently mentioned reasons for becoming business owners were:

- to make a living by working for oneself instead of for others (77 percent)

- to build a business for future income/activity (69 percent)

- to take advantage of a real need/demand for a particular product/-service (51 percent).

The major reasons for choosing their particular businesses were:

- "suited my skills, talents, and/or abilities" (80 percent)

- "I liked the idea of the particular kind of business" (70 percent)

- "I had experience/training in this area" (68 percent)

- "I saw a real need/demand for the product or service" (56 percent).

Interestingly, although 71 percent of the women business owners started their businesses within a year of conceiving the idea and did not spend a great deal of money, only 15 percent saw their venture as a high risk when they started out.

Most women started their businesses with little start-up capital: one-third began with less than $1,000; another 26 percent started with $1,000 to $5,000; and only 3.7 percent had $50,000 or more initial capital. Just over half of the respondents felt that they had enough capital to start their businesses. As to the source of the capital, 74 percent used personal cash and savings. The next most frequently mentioned source of capital was loans from family (23 percent). Among the 308 respondents, 33 had received a commercial business loan and only ten had received a Small Business Administration loan.

The major start-up problems encountered by the women business owners surveyed were: insufficient access to credit and insufficient capital with resulting cash flow problems; building a reputation and advertising effectively; and inadequate record-keeping and financial planning skills. Once started in business, respondents found an ongoing problem in addition to those mentioned to be finding and keeping competent, reliable employees.

Respondents reported having started their first business at an average age of 32. The ages of the owners at the time of the survey ranged from 22 to 70, with an average of 42. Over 80 percent had more than a high school education and 35 percent had a bachelor's or higher degree. Nearly half (47 percent) were single, separated, divorced or widowed, and about one-third (35 percent) had no children; 34 percent had only one or two children. Fifty-eight percent reported a very supportive family reaction, while 20 percent experienced indifference or nonsupport.

The businesses were grouped into three categories according to the owners' interpretations of their current status: struggling/unsuccessful, marginal, or profitable/successful. A significant positive correlation was found between perceived success and gross sales/net profits of the business as well as the owner's personal income. The struggling businesses reported that the following problems were most important: visibility and advertising, motivation, and energy. For the successful businesses, employee relations and completing paperwork/ complying with regulations were the most important.

The report also describes the educational packages designed to assist women entrepreneurs that were developed and used in the program.

Mescon, Timothy and George E. Stevens. "Women As Entrepreneurs: A Preliminary Study of Female Realtors in Arizona." Arizona Business 29, 7 (November 1982): 9-13.

This article presents the results of a survey of women-owned real estate firms in Arizona. Of 309 women selected for the sample only 35 percent responded to the survey questionnaire. Seventy-five percent were married. Twenty percent were divorced. The women in the sample worked long hours. Forty percent worked more than 50 hours a week.

The study utilized the Rotter's Locus of Control Scale to assess these women's belief in their ability to control their own futures. It was found that the respondents tended to have a strong internal locus of control.

In conclusion, the authors argue that women could be more successful in the real estate business if they had previous management experience.

Nelton, Susan. "A Business of Her Own." Nation's Business 72, 11 (November 1984): 70-72.

This article reports on the growth of women-owned businesses, and on steps being taken by the Federal Government to promote entrepreneurship for women. The article cites a recent survey by the National Association of Women Business Owners (NAWBO) which showed that 71 percent of NAWBO members responding were in corporations or partnerships, forms of ownership which tend to be undercounted by the statistics.

The author argues that while statistics show that women are entering business ownership four times as fast as men, they fail to reach their full potential. Although 22 percent of sole proprietorships are owned by women, only 8 percent of such firms' gross receipts and less than 1 percent of federal procurement expenditures go to women. According to Becky Norton Dunlop, the head of the Interagency Committee on Women's Business Enterprise who was interviewed for the article, this situation can be improved if women learn how to enter the federal procurement process.

O'Bannon, Donna. "Women As Entrepreneurs.," Executive 4 (1977): 36-38.

The author argues that women entrepreneurs face staggering obstacles. Most women-owned businesses are concentrated in retail and non-professional services. The typical woman entrepreneur is a sole proprietor with fewer than five employees and less than $51,000 in gross sales. O'Bannon points out that many of the discriminatory problems faced by women entrepreneurs are addressed by the Equal Credit Opportunity Act and subsequent amendments, but women have traditionally been excluded from the networks of local power and referrals that stem from membership in the Rotary, Kiwanis, Jaycees and other social organizations.

Pellegrino, Eric T. and Barry L. Reece. "Perceived Formative and Operational Problems Encountered by Female Entrepreneurs in Retail and Service Firms." Journal of Small Business Management 20 (April 1982): 15-29.

Participants in this study were 25 female entrepreneurs with one or more years' experience in operating a retail or service firm in the Roanoke, Virginia, Standard Metropolitan Statistical Area (SMSA). Described by the authors as "a case study form of descriptive research used to identify the formative and operational problems encountered by female entrepreneurs," the study involved asking women closedand open-ended questions about the formation of their businesses and ongoing operations.

Although a majority indicated they had no serious problems in the formation stage, 25 percent said obtaining funds to start a business was a critical problem. In terms of ongoing operations, record keeping, financial management, and advertising were the areas of greatest concern.

When asked, "Did you encounter any problems in the formative or operational phases of your business that can be attributed partially or wholly to the fact that you are a woman?," a majority answered "no." However, among those who answered "yes," obtaining funds to start and operate the business was most often cited as a problem.

The authors conclude that "the results of this investigation do not give strong support to the contention that female entrepreneurs face special problems in the formation and operation of small business," however, only females were surveyed and, therefore, no empirical comparison is possible.

Proceedings of the National Symposium on Hispanic Business and Economy in the United States, Miami, 1979. Miami: Florida International University, 1980.

The papers in these proceedings focus on the following topics: Hispanic market in the United States, private and government programs, education and training programs, labor force characteristics and consumer trends. Hispanic women in business, business structure and special problems, marketing roundtable, and the Hispanic market in the 1980's.

Resources for Women, Inc. On Their Own: Women Entrepreneurs. Santa Cruz, CA: Resources For Women, Inc., 1979.

Twenty-seven women business owners in Santa Cruz, were interviewed for this book. The women were asked why they went into business, about their backgrounds, and about the financial, legal and psychological aspects of being a women business owner. Community and employee relations are also discussed. Most of the businesses are in the service and retail industries.

Rich-McCoy, Lois. Late Bloomers: Profiles of Women Who Found Their True Calling. New York: Harper & Row, 1980.

This guide encourages women to learn by example from the experiences of others who successfully pursued a new career option or life style later in life. The women profiled started new careers after raising a family, being a homemaker, or being employed in a dead-end job for many years. Biographical profiles were constructed on the basis of interviews with the women's husbands, friends, employees, parents, children, and the women themselves. According to the author, the women "tell their stories and explore their childhoods, marriages, self-images, attitudes toward the feminist movement," and family reactions to their success. Those interviewed include several business owners--a career counselor, two partners in a dress shop, a real estate broker/owner, owners of a home-based travel agency, an architectural/interior design business, and a mail order beauty book and cosmetic business. Other self-employed and professional women are also interviewed.

_____. Millionairess: Self-Made Women of America. New York: Harper & Row, 1978.

The author describes the experiences of 12 "Horatio Alger heroines," women who rose to the top, who neither inherited nor married into wealth, but were financially and professionally successful in their own right. Their personalities, family backgrounds, employment histories, and business experiences are examined. Most of the women profiled are business owners, particularly in manufacturing.

Riggs, C.R. "The Rise of Women Entrepreneurs." D & B Reports (January/-February 1981): 19-23.

This article offers profiles of seven women business owners based on personal interviews. The businesses involved include a management consulting firm, an advertising and public relations agency (one of the nation's top 15), a non-medical home care company, a construction company, a company that sells and services mechanical water equipment (pumps, etc.), and a firm that does wood preserving for guardrails, railway ties, utility poles and other uses.

The women came from different parts of the United States and different backgrounds. Four of the women bought out an existing business from someone else (in two cases from their husbands, following a divorce). They reported their biggest problems were with access to finance and decision-making power groups. All the women belonged to many business and professional groups, but felt that women had little real power. Chambers of Commerce, in particular, were criticized for failing to give positions of responsibility to women. The women argued that the two most important things for the woman business owner are a mentor and a network (a forum for women to communicate as equals, share ideas, make contacts, do business with each other).

Rose, Gerald L. and Arthur D. Brief. "The Status of and Opportunities for Minorities, Women, Aged and Other Special Interest Groups in Small Business." The Regional Environments for Small Business and Entrepreneurship. Washington, D.C.: U. S. Small Business Administration, 1979.

Rose and Brief use secondary sources and a limited mail survey to determine the status of, and opportunities for Region VII's minority and female-owned firms, particularly as related to U.S. patterns.

They conclude that secondary data are generally inadequate for purposes of assessing these groups' current status and future prospects. Both minority group members and females are substantially underrepresented among owners of firms based on their proportions in the populations of Region VII and the nation. The authors conclude that prospects for minorities and females who own businesses are difficult to assess, since there is little adequate information.

The authors recommend establishing special-interest group Business Service Centers with the mission of providing direct services to present and potential minority and female business owners which would include training in the business disciplines, providing equity and operating capital, and assisting in establishing and maintaining relationships with both public and private sector customers.

Scholl, Taye. "The Savvy 60." Savvy (February 1984).

A sort of "Fortune 500" of women-owned businesses, this article highlights successful women business owners and their firms. Thirty businesses are listed with names and addresses of their chief executives. The article also includes some discussion of current issues facing women business owners.

Schreier, James W. "The Female Entrepreneur: A Pilot Study." Milwaukee: Center for Venture Management, 1975.

This is a brief, preliminary study (one of the earliest), on the personal histories and personality characteristics of the female entrepreneur, published by the now-defunct Center for Venture Management. The study presents the results of personal interviews of women business owners conducted in Milwaukee. The sample of 14 was selected from among "several women known to be owners of their own businesses," names obtained through unspecified published references, and personal contact with various women's and business organizations.

The study focuses on women in business areas that are typically male dominated (including many service-related businesses, but not "typically female" service businesses such as beauty shops). The resulting profile of women entrepreneurs was compared to earlier research on male entrepreneurs. According to the author, the survey results showed that women entrepreneurs were similar to their male counterparts in: impetus for starting their businesses (economic necessity or seized opportunity), family history (entrepreneurial father who had great influence on them), and willingness to accept risk.

However, the women differed from their male counterparts in their attitudes toward education and working for others. Women generally did not mind working for others. Research indicates that the opposite is usually true for male entrepreneurs.

On the basis of this study Schreier concluded that there were no significant differences between male and female entrepreneurs.

The study is limited by its reliance on a small and non-random sample, the author's failure to justify the use of discriminatory variables and lack of a control group of male entrepreneurs or female non-entrepreneurs for comparison. However, the study was never intended to be more then a pilot, written to encourage further research on women business owners. Its faults are ones that are common to many studies of women entrepreneurs.

Schwartz, E.B. "Entrepreneurship: A New Female Frontier." Journal of Contemporary Business 5 (Winter 1976): 47-76.

This 1976 study compares findings of a survey of 20 female entrepreneurs with results of research on male entrepreneurs as reported in the literature from 1958 to 1975. Major findings include:

- the major motivations for entering business were similar for male and female entrepreneurs--the need to achieve, desire to be independent, need for job satisfaction and economic necessity

- women tend to have an autocratic management style. They closely watch and control their businesses. (This is also characteristic of men in the first stages of their companies' growth)

- the women felt the major barrier they faced was credit discrimination in the capital formation stage of business development

The author did not find many differences in the characteristics of male and female entrepreneurs. The sample size was too small to draw any major conclusions about the characteristics of the overall population of female entrepreneurs.

Scott, G. "Women Retailers Mean Business." <u>Black Enterprise</u> 9 (May 1979): 43-45.

The author notes that "Black women have always been an integral part of black efforts toward economic self-reliance." Black women retailers now account for 21.8 percent of black retailers. In this article three retail businesses owned by black women were selected at random and the owners interviewed. Their clothing stores are located in Minneapolis, Minnesota, Jackson, Mississippi, and Beverly Hills, California. Brief accounts of the women and the development of their businesses are offered.

Sexton, Donald and Calvin Kent. "Female Executives and Entrepreneurs: A Preliminary Comparison." <u>Frontiers of Entrepreneurship Research: Proceedings, 1983 Conference on Entrepreneurship</u> (Babson College, 1983).

The authors compared female executives and entrepreneurs utilizing a sample of 45 executives and 48 entrepreneurs, all residing and conducting business in Texas. The results indicated that female entrepreneurs and executives tend to be more similar than different. Comparisons were also made between the results of this study and previous investigations which attempted to characterize entrepreneurs and contrast them with executives.

The two groups were compared with respect to the following variables:

- sibling position--the majority of both groups were middle children or born last (in contrast to the findings of Hennig and Jardim that showed women executives were generally eldest children-see appendix for citation)

- motivation--job satisfaction and professional recognition were most often cited by both

- parent's occupation--the father's occupation had a stronger influence on the entrepreneurs (confirming a prominent theory of entrepreneurship) than on the executives

- education--was slightly higher for the executives (supporting a commonly held notion that entrepreneurs enter business ownership because they lack proper credentials for management in a firm owned by someone else), but the younger entrepreneurs had more education than the younger executives

- work experience--the entrepreneurs changed jobs more than the executives, but a majority of both said their current occupation was directly related to previous work

- personal priorities--the entrepreneurs rated job first, family second; the executives just the opposite

- principle ingredient of success--the executives believed that working with people was most important, followed by hard work; the entrepreneurs found persistence to be most important, followed by hard work and working with people

- self concept--both saw themselves as "doers", and the propensity for risk taking was almost identical for both groups. Although many scholars feel this is an important aspect of entrepreneurship, other research has also shown that a high degree of risk taking is not a significant characteristic of entrepreneurs.

This study suffers from the following limitations: small sample size did not allow for comparison of female entrepreneurs and executives by type of industry and by size of firm; the sample was not randomly drawn; and different survey methods were used for the two groups. However, the authors readily acknowledge these drawbacks, and in spite of them the study is a valuable one. The main features that recommend it are its use of a comparative methodology and its attempts to relate findings to other work in the field of entrepreneurship research.

Sheppard, Nathaniel. "Women's Work." Black Enterprise 11 (February 1981): 57-58, 61-62.

The author reviews information about women business owners from the 1977 census and offers recommendations for improving opportunities for women in business. He argues that most women in business feel that, despite the problems, business ownership is more appealing than a dead-end job. Some of the suggestions given for women include: be willing to invest money up front, be prepared to work harder and longer than a man and to adhere to a different set of societal rules, and throughly research the area interested. It is argued that government assistance to women business owners has improved, but is still inadequate, especially in government procurement.

Shook, Robert L. The Entrepreneurs: Twelve Who Took Risks and Succeeded. New York: Harper & Row, 1980.

The individuals profiled in this book were all "self-made successes." A review of these stories provides inspiration for would-be entrepreneurs and a guide to business tactics which can and do work. Two women entrepreneurs are included in the book: Mary Hudson Hudson Oil Company, and Mary Kay Ash of Mary Kay Cosmetics, Inc.

Small Business Development Program, University of New Hampshire. Directory of Women-Owned Businesses in New Hampshire 1982. Durham, N.H.: Small Business Development Program, University of New Hampshire, 1982.

This directory contains an appendix (pp. 118-130) with detailed results of a survey of women business owners in New Hampshire, as well as some comparative information on men business owners in the state who were surveyed at the same time.

The survey result showed that the majority of the respondents to the survey of women-owned businesses in New Hampshire were concentrated in retail trade (36 percent) and services (16 percent). Over 70 percent of these businesses had less than five employees and nearly half had gross receipts of less than $100,000. The tabulation of survey results also contains information about initial and ongoing finance, education, experience and perceived business problems as reported by the women surveyed.

Small Business Secretariat, Policy Research and Formulation Unit. Canadian Women Owner/Managers. Ottowa: Government of Canada, 1982.

A review of the Canadian Taxation Statistics showed that the number of women business proprietors was increasing faster than the number of men business proprietors. Women own one-fifth of those proprietorships with taxable income and one-third of all proprietorships (including those with and without taxable income). However, the women proprietors have much lower earnings.

This document also reports on a study carried out by Queen's University in Ontario. Some 275 women business owner/managers in Southern Ontario were surveyed. Their names were obtained from a list provided by the Dun and Bradstreet Corporation. The study showed that: most of the women had started their own businesses rather than inheriting or buying them; most owned relatively young businesses; the businesses tended to be relatively large employers, especially of women; very few were in franchising; many of the owners had entrepreneurial family backgrounds; challenge was the most important motivational factor; and most felt the problems faced by women business owners were no different from those faced by men business owners.

The paper also reviews the results of the 1972 U.S. Census of Women Business Owners, the Report of the President's Task Force on Women Business Owners and the study by Schwartz.

Smith, Norman, Gary McCain, and Audrey Warren. "Women Entrepreneurs Really Are Different: A Comparison of Constructed Ideal Types of Male and Female Entrepreneurs." Frontiers of Entrepreneurship Research: Proceedings, 1983 Conference on Entrepreneurship. (Babson College, 1982).

The study is based on 76 responses to a survey of female entrepreneurs in the San Francisco area (all members of a women entrepreneurs organization). The behavior and attitudes of the women were analyzed using a scale developed to evaluate entrepreneurial types. The scale used classified entrepreneurs within a range bounded by two extreme types: craft-oriented (rigid) and opportunistic (adaptable). In a comparison of the results of this study with the authors' previous study of male entrepreneurs, it was found that female entrepreneurs were different from their male counterparts; specifically, they tended to be more opportunistic.

"Special Problems and Advantages of Women Business Owners." Professional Report 10 (January 1980): 17-19.

The article points out that more and more women are entering business. The author argues that women may face problems of discrimination and fear of risk when they start. Also included is a discussion of government assistance for women business owners through Small Business Administration loans and federal procurement.

Strang, William A. Wisconsin Restaurant Survey. Madison: University of Wisconsin, Small Business Development Center, 1980.

This report on the restaurant industry in Wisconsin contains some information on women-owned businesses in that industry (p. 25 of the report), which represent 18 percent of the total. The report is based on data generated by a 1979 sample survey of 1,000 restaurants drawn from listings in telephone directories.

Strang, William A. and James F. McConnell. The 1980 Wisconsin Beauty/ Barber Shop Survey. Madison: University of Wisconsin, Small Business Development Center, 1981.

This report is based on the results of a 1980 survey of approximately 1,000 beauty and barber shops in the state of Wisconsin. The brief discussion of women business owners in that industry reveals that they represent 48 percent of beauty/barber shop owners in the state and tend to have larger shops in terms of number of employees and square footage. However, there was no significant difference in gross sales by gender of owner (see pp. 22-24 of the report).

Struggs, Callie Foster. Women In Business. Mesquita, TX: Ide House, 1981.

Although this short essay deals mainly with women as business executives, one chapter on women entrepreneurs attempts to link together the problems of women in the labor force in general with those of women in management and women business owners. The arguments are supported by extensive references to appropriate statistics. The appendix contains tables on education of women, earnings of women executives, and laws related to the prohibition of sex discrimination.

Trescott, Martha Moore Scott, ed. Dynamos and Virgins Revisited: Women and Technological Change in History: An Anthology. Metuchen, NJ: Scarecrow Press, 1979.

This book collects some of the more significant works on the interaction between women and technology. It contains eleven scholarly essays, and is designed as a reference tool and a text for courses on women's history and other women's studies, history of science and technology, economic and business history, and other related areas. Both European and American topics, from the 18th century to the 20th, are included, although the focus is on the United States in the last hundred years.

The readings in Part I treat women as active participants in technological change, focusing on women operatives in industry and women inventors, engineers, scientists and entrepreneurs.

U.S. Department of Labor. National Commission on the Observance of International Women's Year, 1976. "...To Form a More Perfect Union..." Justice for American Women. Washington, D.C.: U.S. Department of Labor, 1977.

This report discusses the obstacles to equal rights for women and deals with varied economic and social issues. There is a brief discussion of the woman entrepreneur (pp. 61-64) as well as an analysis of issues that affect the woman business owner, such as credit access, women in the labor force and the family responsibilities of women.

_____. The Spirit of Houston. Washington, D.C.: U. S. Government Printing Office, 1978.

This report on the First National Women's Conference in Houston contains a two-page discussion of women in business (pp. 22-23) and recommendations for changes in government policies in order to provide greater assistance for women business owners. The major recommendation is that women be included in the Small Business Administration's subcontracting program (the "8-a" program, so-called because its authority stems from section 8-a of the Small Business Act).

U.S. Interagency Committee on Women's Business Enterprise. Annual Report to the President. Washington, D.C.: U.S. Small Business Administration, 1980.

The Interagency Committee on Women's Business Enterprise was specifically charged with overseeing the development, coordination and implementation of the national program for women's business enterprise, preparing a joint federal and private sector plan to increase the number of women-owned businesses and promoting the growth and success of existing ones.

The report describes the activities of the Interagency Committee in the first year following the issuance of Executive Order 12138. It outlines the progress made by the Federal Government in addressing the problems of women business owners as directed by the order. The report also reviews the problems women business owners face, and suggests the future direction the Federal Government and the private sector should take to bring women further into the mainstream of business ownership. A series of goals for the next five years is outlined. Particularly emphasized are financial access, opening new markets, and management assistance for women business owners; data collection, analysis and research; and ways to increase public awareness of government programs available to women business owners.

U.S. President's Interagency Task Force on Women Business Owners. The Bottom Line: Unequal Enterprise in America. Washington, D.C.: U.S. Government Printing Office, 1978.

In August 1977, President Carter established an Interagency Task Force on Women Business Owners which included high level representatives from eight federal agencies. The Task Force report, submitted to the President in June of 1978, is based on a thorough review of the information and literature on women business owners, their businesses and business problems available at the time. The Task Force mandate included the identification and assessment of existing data on women entrepreneurs, and the assessment of federal programs and practices that might have an impact on women entrepre- neurs.

In addition, the report includes the results of a nationwide survey of about 3,000 women business owners. Distribution of the survey instrument was accomplished through public service announcements, notice to universities and women's resource centers and organizations, and the regional offices of the Department of Commerce and the Small Business Administration. A total of 27,000 questionnaires were distributed, of which 3,454 were returned in time for processing. Of these, 2,973 were from women business owners. The results of that survey are presented and analyzed in the report. The data indicated that the respondents:

- were employed for several years before starting their own businesses

- initiated their own businesses and did not inherit them

- were interested in being independent

- started their own businesses alone, and without assistance

- were married and had a family

- were motivated by the desire for money, and to use their unique skills and talents

- were daughters of a parent who had been self-employed and mothers who were employed outside the home

- had initiated their businesses within the last 10 years.

Because of the way responses were solicited, the respondents do not constitute a representative sample of the population of women business owners as a whole and the findings may not be extrapolated.

The Task Force Report addresses the following topics in considerable detail: the changing status of women in the work force and its relationship to women's enterprise development; assessment of available data on women-owned businesses and their proprietors; education and women's entrepreneurship; management training and technical assistance for women business owners; capital formation and credit for women in business, (including federal loan and grant programs); women and the government market; and legislative and regulatory barriers to women's business ownership.

Extensive recommendations for improving government policies and programs to better assist the woman business owner are included. A glossary, bibliography and statistical appendices are also provided.

U.S. Small Business Administration. The State of Small Business: A Report of the President. Washington, D.C. U.S. Government Printing Office, various years.

Released annually since 1982, The State of Small Business provides extensive information on all aspects of the small business economy. Each edition of the report contains an appendix or chapter which provides a ready source of data on women business owners and their businesses.

The 1985 edition reports an SBA estimate of 3 million women-owned businesses for 1984. This estimate was based on published and unpublished figures from the Internal Revenue Service and the SBA's Ownership Characteristics Survey of the small business owners in its Small Business Data Base, which was conducted during 1984. The report also discusses trends in the industrial distribution, business receipts, and government procurement activity of women-owned businesses.

Welsch, Harold P. and Earl C. Young. "Women At the Top." Management World 12, 8 (September 1983): 32.

This article summarizes the findings presented in two earlier papers by the authors, in which they investigated differences and similarities between male and female entrepreneurs and found that women used more written sources of information than men, and were more realistic in their assessments of economic conditions than men. Among those surveyed, the volume of sales was lower for women ($100,000 - $200,000) than for men ($200,000 - $300,000). The women tended to have more education, but less business experience. Women's reasons for going into business and the advantages and problems of business ownership for women also were discussed.

White, Jerry. "The Rise of Female Capitalism--Women as Entrepreneurs." Business Quarterly 49, 1 (Spring 1984): 133-36.

The results of a 1978 survey of 1,989 new businesses in Canada, and a follow-up survey in 1981 indicate that over a three year period, 47 percent of the 1,364 ventures owned by women were still in business, whereas only 25 percent of the 486 male-owned firms were still operating. The author suggests that women are becoming a powerful force in Canadian small business, and may be more successful in surviving economic downturns than their male counterparts. The study also found that women tend to use their own finances. Therefore, financial marketers might profit from better targeting toward women. The author's conclusions call on professional firms, business publications, and government agencies to provide increased attention to the needs of female entrepreneurs.

Williams, Constance H. The Women's Project. Philadelphia: Small Business Development Center, The University of Pennsylvania, 1982.

The Women's Project of the Wharton Small Business Development Center (SBDC) was created to test the hypothesis that specific problems do exist for women small business owners which are not common to small business owners in general.

In three focus group sessions, the Wharton Small Business Development Center interviewed 18 women who owned or were starting their own businesses. From these conversations the author identified three specific areas in which women small business owners had different problems than men: in their approach to the financial aspects of the business, in their sense of isolation and need for networking, and in the multiple demands that business and family responsibilities made on their time.

The study team then surveyed a larger sample (300) of women business owners to test the strength of the problem areas identified by the focus groups. The majority of the 130 respondents felt that in most business skill areas women business owners did not have different or greater problems than men. However, 45 percent thought it was more difficult for women to obtain loans than for men. In terms of personal characteristics and social constraints, a majority said women entrepreneurs had different problems than men had. Half of the respondents believed men do not take women business owners seriously.

The final report explains the methodology involved in running the focus groups, identifies the population base from which the participants were chosen, and presents a summary of the most significant responses organized by topic. It next discusses the survey questionnaire and its results. Based on the results of the survey, possible new programs for the center are suggested.

"Women at Work: AMA Survey Shows How and Why Females Succeed As Business Owners." Management Review 67 (November 1978): 56.

A one-page article that appeared as a part of Management Review's regular column, "Research Spotlight". Highlights the major findings of the AMA survey of successful women business owners, which was undertaken in conjunction with the work of the President's Interagency Task Force on Women Business Owners in 1978.

"Women Rise as Entrepreneurs." Business Week (Industrial Edition) 625 (February 25, 1980): 85-86, 91.

This article argues that, although women have traditionally played a minor role in the creation of new business enterprises, a change is coming as the number of female entrepreneurs increases and their operating styles change. The article points out that although more women have advanced degrees and management experience and are moving aggressively into high technology and manufacturing businesses, the majority of the businesses are on the low end of the small business scale. All encounter the obstacles of dealing with a predominantly male banking and financial community and with nervous vendors and customers. Relatively few female entrepreneurs have attracted venture capital. The authors argue that attitudes may change as women reach barriers to career advancement within corporations and opt to start their own business.

The article also mentions government programs to train and finance potential women business owners. However, it is pointed out that successful women entrepreneurs feel that women must learn to be less conservative, to take more risks, and to adjust to the demands which will affect their family and personal lives.

Unpublished Dissertations, Papers and Manuscripts

Bloom, H. and Margaret T. Shaffer. "Women-Owned Businesses: A Concept Paper." Potomac, MD: Paradigm, Inc., 1978. Mimeographed.

This study begins with a review of the data on women-owned businesses. At the time it was written the only major sources available were the 1972 census and self-employment data from the Bureau of Labor Statistics.

The second part of the paper examines the interaction between women's participation in the labor force and entrepreneurship for women. The authors note that only a very slow movement from the traditional job picture is projected for the future. Business opportunities and jobs for women will still be focused largely in areas with low economic viability and little mobility. In 1976, 78.7 percent of the clerical workers were women, but only 20.8 percent of managerial and administrative workers were women (and that figure included food service workers and sales managers in retail trade). It is suggested that one motive women have for starting their own businesses is their inability to advance in their present job. Thus women form new enterprises in order to allow themselves the upward mobility not offered by the corporate structure.

The authors assert that occupational segregation of women workers limits the options and success of the potential women entrepreneur by narrowing the fields she may choose to enter, depriving her of management skills and knowledge, and reducing her ability to accumulate the collateral and management track record necessary for starting a business. In addition, because of this situation in the labor force, women lack the confidence in their own capability and credibility that they need to start, conduct and be successful in a business. As changes slowly occur in the work force women will have new ideas and options, and the authors feel one of those will be business ownership.

The paper also discusses the impact of recent legislation and government programs on women, especially on those who own businesses. Finally, an approach to marketing high technology communications equipment to women business owners is outlined.

DeCarlo, James F. and Paul R. Lyons. "Characteristics of Successful Female Entrepreneurs." Frostburg, MD: Frostburg State College, 1978. Mimeographed.

DeCarlo and Lyons attempt to apply the EPPS (Edwards Personal Preference Schedule) and SIV (Gordon Survey of Interpersonal Values) tests, that were used by Hornaday and Aboud (see Appendix) in studying male entrepreneurs, to successful female entrepreneurs in order to compare the two groups. A "successful" entrepreneur was defined by Hornaday and Aboud as one who had spent at least five years as head of an operating business in the mid-Atlantic region, and was of the average age of 45.

The differences in personality characteristics between male and female entrepreneurs, as measured by the SIV and EPPS tests, were found to be very slight and generally insignificant. Differences in personality characteristics between entrepreneurs and the female population in general were found to be quite large and significant.

The female entrepreneurs in the sample differed from the men in Hornaday and Aboud's study in that the women had fewer employees, had less experience in business, worked fewer hours, had a higher frequency of separation and divorce, had less education and were less accepting of regimentation. However, DeCarlo and Lyons argued that some of the differences found may be related to the type of business the women were operating--but their sample size was not large enough to allow testing of this hypothesis.

_____. "An Exploratory Analysis of Job and Life Satisfaction Among Entrepreneurs." Frostburg, MD: Frostburg State College, n.d. Mimeographed. ERIC Document #ED226134.

This paper is described as "a pilot study to examine the concepts of job satisfaction and life satisfaction among a sample of female entrepreneurs." A sample of 32 female entrepreneurs from Maryland, Pennsylvania, and West Virginia was compared to a sample of 32 "bureaucratic" females (in this case, nursing supervisors at three hospitals in New Jersey and Maryland). Questionnaries based on the Job Description Index (JDI) were administered, along with global measures of job and life satisfaction. The results showed that female entrepreneurs scored higher on the "work" and "people" scales of the JDI, but lower on the "pay" scale. However, only the work scale difference was significant. The entrepreneurs scored higher than the supervisors on the global measures of job and life satisfaction, but these differences were not statistically significant.

One cannot conclude from this study that there are any significant differences in job and life satisfaction between female entrepreneurs and "bureaucratic" females. Such a conclusion is not supported by the results of the statistical tests actually made. Furthermore, even if the tests applied had showed significant differences to exist, it is unlikely that the results could be generalized to female populations in question. First, nurse supervisors may not be an adequate proxy for "bureaucratic" females. There might be any number of other variables that would better explain their level of job and life satisfaction when compared to that of female entrepreneurs.

Demarest, Janice Lyski. "Women Minding Their Own Businesses: A Pilot Study of Independent Business and Professional Women and Their Enterprises." Unpublished Ph.D. Dissertation, University of Colorado, 1977.

Demarest interviewed 51 women business owners and independent professionals on a wide range of topics, including attitudes toward success; risk-taking and competition; goals and levels of aspiration; identification of their strengths, weaknesses, and accomplishments in relation to conventional notions of masculinity and femininity; and the integration of their enterprises with family and personal lives. Although most of the women business owners interviewed were confident in their ability to succeed when they initiated their businesses, approximately 50 percent indicated an increase in confidence since initiating their businesses. Other ways they believed having their own businesses had changed them included: greater ambition or goal orientation; increased knowledge and greater competence; and a stronger sense of self-reliance, independence and self-respect.

Most women in the survey wanted to improve the operations of their businesses rather than expand. The following three approaches to business operation were used by the women business owners: a competitive approach, a non-competitive approach which stressed quality of work, and a refusal to admit the existence of any competition. Of the women in the non-competitive group, 25 percent expressed this quality in "feminine" terms and stated that they did better work because of the fact that they were women.

Regarding attitudes toward risk taking, more than 60 percent indicated little or no worry about financial risks involved in operating their enterprises. Very few risked large sums of money, and many had other means of financial support.

Evans, David. "Entrepreneurial Choice and Success." Study prepared for the Office of Veteran's Affairs, U.S. Small Business Administration. Greenwich, CT: CERA Economic Consultants, Inc., 1985.

In the United States today, there are a total of approximately 9 million self-employed workers, representing about 9 percent of the work force. This study relies on data drawn from the 1970 and 1980 Public Use Sample of the U.S. Bureau of the Census to compare characteristics of wage and salary workers and the self-employed. Although longitudinal data would have allowed for a richer analysis, there are too few self-employed workers in the National Longitudinal Samples to allow for reliable statistical analysis.

The study's sample excludes self-employed professionals (such as doctors and lawyers) and farmers, all workers under the age of 18 or over the age of 65, and those who work less than 36 hours a week or less than 40 weeks per year. All self-employed workers in the Public Use Sample that were not excluded by the above restrictions were included in the study's sample. Of wage and salary workers, 15 percent were randomly selected from the 1970 Public Use Sample and eight from 1980. According to Census figures, only about 4 percent of women and 10 percent of men who meet the criteria for inclusion in the study's sample were self-employed in 1980. The study sample included 7,275 males (3,032 self-employed) and 2,392 women (488 self-employed) for 1970, and 6,205 males (3,735 self-employed) and 2,237 females (833 self-employed) for 1980.

The study examined characteristics of men and women separately because of differences in labor market behavior between the two groups. It found that self-employed women were older and had less college education than female wage and salary workers. In addition, there were fewer blacks and more immigrants among self-employed women than among female wage and salary workers.

Flesher, D.L. and K.W. Hollman. "A Profile of Women, the Elderly, and Minority Persons in Small Business." The Environment for Entrepreneurship and Small Business in the Regions. Washington, D.C.: U.S. Small Business Administration, 1981.

The primary purpose of this study, one of a series commissioned by the U.S. Small Business Administration, was to characterize females, elderly persons, and persons from minority groups who own or manage small businesses in the South. This purpose was achieved through an investigation of their social origins, educational background, career routes and other relevant information.

A sample of 1,000 small business owners and managers was obtained from the Small Business Administration, Business and Professional Women's Clubs, black business organizations, Service Corps of Retired Executives (SCORE) chapters, and directories of manufacturing and retailing industries in Mississippi, Georgia, Kentucky, Tennessee, Florida, South Carolina, North Carolina, and Alabama. The owners and managers were surveyed by questionnaire and personal interview.

When responses were compared, "the statistics showed that the typical small business woman is slightly younger than the male, is more apt to be unmarried, more likey to have had clerical, sales or teaching experience, and has slightly less managerial experience before assuming her present position. Her husband has probably been instrumental in her decision to start a small business. One of the most common motivating factors was the desire to have time available when needed by family members, particularly children."

The major drawback of this paper as a study of women entrepreneurs is that the sample includes both owners and managers of small businesses with no distinction made between the two groups.

Flexman, N.A. "Women of Enterprise: A Study of Success and Failure Incidents From Self-Employed Women Using the Perspectives of Bakan's Constructs of Agency and Communion and Attribution Theory." Unpublished Ph.D. Dissertation, University of Illinois, 1980.

The purpose of the study was to investigate how self-employed women interpret the entrepreneurial experience. Data were collected by personal interviews with 61 self-employed women. Each woman was asked to describe her business experience and to answer questions regarding three success and three failure incidents related to their business. Stepwise multiple regression analysis resulted in an equation which included five predictor variables: ability, communion, intelligence, religious faith, and confidence. These five predictors accounted for 77 percent of the variation. Success incidents could be predicted by high scores on the five predictor variables, while failure incidents could be predicted by low scores.

Harris, John B. "Status and Opportunities for Minorities, Women and the Aged (Region III)." The Environment for Entrepreneurship and Small Business in the Regions. Washington, D.C.: U.S. Small Business Administration, 1979.

This report contains information on the number and types of business loans going to women-owned firms in Region VII in fiscal years 1974, 1975, and 1976. Women received 7 percent of the number of loans and guarantees approved in 1974, 9 percent in 1975, and 11 percent in 1976. But when computed in terms of the dollar amount, the percentages of loans and guarantees that went to women were lower in each year.

Hisrich, Robert D. and Candida Brush. "Women Entrepreneurs: Present Skills and Outlook for the Future." Boston College, 1982, Mimeographed.

This paper is a report on a nationwide survey of women business owners conducted by the authors in 1982. Of 1,151 owners contacted, 468 responded to a questionnaire about their businesses, backgrounds, skills and needs for assistance.

The majority of the women had been employed in service occupations before starting their own businesses, but gave themselves relatively high ratings with respect to management skills. The women rated their financial skills weakest and listed insufficient business training and lack of finance and working capital as their biggest problems. They generally expressed concern about the lack of role models and acceptance of women as business owners, especially in non-traditional areas such as manufacturing and construction. Many stated that they had trouble getting men to accept them as competent and serious business owners. They felt that women's attitudes had to change as well, to demonstrate more self-confidence and assertiveness. Tables are provided.

Ito, Barbara Darlington. "Entrepreneurial Women in Urban Japan: The Role of Personal Networks." Unpublished Ph.D. Dissertation, University of Iowa, 1983.

This anthropology dissertation is a study of women entrepreneurs in Nihama City, a port city of approximately 130,000 people on the Island of Shikoku. The major emphasis is placed on socialization of Japanese women and networking, although employment opportunities are also discussed. Extensive background information is provided on family life, the role of daughters, education, and marriage in urban Japan.

Businesses operated by women are divided into three types: businesses in which a self-employed woman exercises primary control over all aspects of the business; family businesses in which women play an active role in management and operation; and commission sales activities. Of the women interviewed for the dissertation, only three owned large businesses--two had inherited a business from their husbands and the third built the business herself. Most of the women studied were involved in small-scale service and retail businesses. Their start-up funds generally came from personal savings or loans from family and friends. However, women in family businesses usually inherited the business or entered it through their husbands' families. Of the three groups, the self-employed women tended to have less education.

Iwao, Sumiko. "Skills and Life Strategies of Japanese Business Women." Paper from the Bernard VanLeer Foundation Project on Human Potential. Cambridge, MA: Gutman Library, Harvard School of Education, 1984. ERIC Document #ED254465.

The author argues that traditional Japanese female values-- thrift, industriousness, harmony, avoidance of conflict, and empathy--are conducive to successful business ownership. This conclusion is illustrated by two cases, women who were chosen as "representative" from a sample of 56 Japanese women business owners. The paper does not describe how the original "sample" of 56 was selected.

The first case presented was of a woman restaurant owner who had inherited her business. The restaurant business is one in which Japanese women traditionally take an active role, particularly in giving individual attention to guests. The second woman had started her own firm, an importing company for veterinary pharmaceuticals. This woman had some familiarity with this type of business because her father had owned one in a similar line. Both women reported reluctance to expand their businesses or engage in further risk-taking. They felt they were not discriminated against because they were women, and had experienced little difficulty in acquiring bank loans.

The author argues that the strength of Japanese women business owners is in personnel management, particularly because of their disposition toward harmony and avoidance of conflict. He claims that women pay more attention to detail and interpersonal relations, have a higher propensity to save, but are less apt to expand their businesses than are men.

Lopes, Marguerite, Janice View and June Sekera. Women, Welfare and Enterprise. Washington, D.C.: American Enterprise Institute, 1983.

A report for a 1983 conference on women, welfare and enterprise by the Neighborhood Revitalization Project of the American Enterprise Institute. The first background paper presented in the report challenges many commonly held views about women and welfare. A second paper addresses a number of issues related to women's business ownership. It explores the reasons for limited female entrepreneurship and suggests steps that can be taken to increase the rate of business formation by women, including among low-income women and those on welfare. Although the background studies present an excellent discussion of both welfare problems and women's business ownership, they are weakest in their attempt to link the two subjects. The conference proceedings summarized in this publication attempt to make these linkages more clear. Recommendations for changes in government policy and programs are included.

Lornes, Millicent. "A Study of the Existence of Selected Characteristics that May Be Necessary For Entrepreneurial Success Among Black Female College Students Majoring in Business." Unpublished Ph.D., Dissertation. Vanderbilt University, 1981.

This study outlines the personal characteristics which enhance success in entrepreneurship and investigates the existence of these characteristics among black women majoring in business at the undergraduate level. The scores of female and male participants were compared with norms for business executives using the California Psychological Inventory (CPI). Black females in the study self-scored significantly lower than the business executive norm and below the general population norm on the scales of: status, sense of well-being, responsibility, socialization, self-control, tolerance, communality, achievement via conformity, achievement via independence, intellectual efficiency, good impression, and psychological mindedness. The black females surveyed differed significantly from the black males surveyed on only three scales--females scored lower on the good impression scale and higher on the achievement via independence and femininity scales.

Based on the research findings, the author recommends that training for black women interested in entrepreneurship should include assertiveness training, self-awareness and self-discovery methodologies, decision-making skills, stress alleviation techniques and organizing skills.

This study should be considered as preliminary exploratory research on the entrepreneurship training needs of black women. The restricted nature of the sample makes it difficult to generalize about the needs of black women entrepreneurs as a whole.

Lustgarten, Steven & Associates. "Financial Success and Business Ownership Among Vietnam and Other Veterans." Office of Economic Research, U.S. Small Business Administration. Washington, D.C.: 1985.

Although the focus of this study is not women business owners per se, there is a section which compares the self-employment rates and "business success" of women (both veterans and non-veterans), and of male and female veterans. Objectives of the research were to determine whether select groups (e.g., male and female) of veterans have more difficulty than others (male and female non-veterans who own businesses) in achieving "financial success"; and to determine whether any lack of financial success may be due to differences in age, time since discharge, education or other environmental factors.

Methven, Susanne Barbara. "Women Owners of Small Businesses." Thesis, Hollins College, VA: 1978.

An honors thesis that raises many critical issues related to women's business ownership, including socialization of women and their position in the labor force and in management. The paper also contains a review of the entrepreneurship literature as it relates to women. The latter half of the paper is a study of women entrepreneurs in the Washington, D.C. area based on a survey of women whose businesses were listed in an area directory.

Morris, Nancy Jo. "Women Apparel Shop Owners: Definitive Profiles and Selected Characteristics." Ph.D. Dissertation, Oklahoma State University, 1984.

This study of women business owners/operators of retail clothing stores -- a type of business in which women have traditionally been actively involved. The study explores relationships between form of ownership, size of store, type of merchandise, length of ownership, and the degree of control and participation in the operation of the store by its owner. The findings are based on the responses of 108 female store owners who responded to a questionnaire sent to a random sample of attendees at a business workshop conducted by the Oklahoma State University's Center for Apparel Marketing and Merchandising.

Of the respondents, 45 percent were sole proprietors and 17 percent were partners in their businesses. The majority of respondents' businesses had annual sales of less than $200,000. Sources of start-up finance included personal savings (for one-third of the respondents) and bank loans (39 percent). The author found that those women who had owned their businesses for longer periods of time and those who owned the larger stores tended to be less involved in the day-to-day management of their stores but continued to be very active in making policy decisions.

National Association of Women Business Owners. "NAWBO Membership Profile." Study conducted under a grant from the Office of Women's Business Ownership, U.S. Small Business Administration. Chicago: National Association of Women Business Owners, 1984.

The National Association of Women Business Owners (NAWBO) conducted a survey of its 1,287 members in January of 1984. The findings of that survey, based on the responses of 766 members, are reported mainly in tabular form. Some background information on how the survey was conducted is provided in this document.

One major finding of the survey was the larger size of NAWBO firms, as compared to the size of women-owned businesses reported by the Internal Revenue Service and the Bureau of the Census. The NAWBO survey respondents' firms had combined total revenues of over $500 million per year. The average yearly revenues of their companies was $425,000, and 75 percent of those surveyed has gross annual sales of over $80,000. In contrast, the average yearly revenues of female-operated sole proprietorships reported by the IRS was only $13,333. However, NAWBO surveyed only its membership and did not employ sampling techiques, while the IRS figures report on millions of businesses, many of which are very small. In addition, according to this survey, some 60 percent of the NAWBO respondents owned partnerships or corporations, while 100 percent of the firms represented by the IRS data are sole proprietorships.

The study also reports that NAWBO members' firms employed an average of 11 full-time and 14 part-time or contractual workers. Over three-fourths of the owners worked 40 hours or more per week, and 28 percent worked 60 hours or more. The great majority of respondents (79 percent) had started their own firms, and 44 percent had been in business for more than five years.

Financial planning was cited by respondents as a key area in which they required assistance. Other areas included: marketing/promotion, hiring the right staff, delegation of authority, personnel development, and long-range strategic planning.

This study is significant because it is the first to examine the characteristics of the only national membership-based trade organization specifically of and for women business owners.

National Business League. "Minority Women in Business." Report prepared for the U.S. Small Business Administration. Washington, D.C.: Office of Women's Business Ownership, 1981.

This report seeks to determine the key factors, beyond sex, which may inhibit the successful establishment and growth of enterprises owned by black and other minority women. Data were collected from 426 women-owned firms by National Business League representatives in 13 geographical areas. Mailed questionnaires as well as persona interviews were used to collect information. Over 94 percent of the respondents were black, 4.5 percent were Hispanic, and 1 percent were classified as "other." Most were married (65 percent). Over half (56 percent) of the respondents had been in business for at least five years. A large proportion were incorporated and most were employers (50 percent) who had four employees or more. Commercial banks were the source of financing for 53 percent of the women. Only 32 percent listed family and friends as the major source of capital. Most had not done business with state and local governments.

Respondents saw racism and jurisdictional location as the primary barriers to succes in business, and identified the following additional barriers as significant:

● fear for personal safety

● attitudinal problems in both the public and private sectors

● stereotypes which differentiate between black and white women

● lack of black females who have entrepreneurial backgrounds in important positions within federal programs designed to assist the woman business owner

● perception that competition in the market place for minority women business owners is confined to competition with white female business owners

- inadequate capital, advertising and market competition were also listed as major factors inhibiting business success of the respondents

The primary weakness of the study are the selection of the sample of business owners to be surveyed (sample selection was non-random, and the details of selection are unknown), and the use of different survey instruments for different participants.

Nielsen, Lucille H. "An Explanatory-Descriptive Study of Mid-Life Women Who Have Created First-Time Independent Businesses." Ph.D. Dissertation, University of Oregon, 1981.

An investigation of the attitudes and behaviors of middle-aged women who had created their first independent businesses. The sample consisted of 16 women business owners from the Eugene, Oregon area. Using a case study approach, the author sought to explore characteristics of the group of women interviewed, as well as trends and insights unique to each individual. The six major factors investigated were: motivation, stress, the role and nature of supportive relationships, educational patterns, work and leisure interests, inner- vs. outer-directedness, and future potential. The interviewing instruments used included: a personal fact data sheet, interview schedule emphasizing the mid-life stage, and the (Shostrom) Personal Orientation Inventory.

The author found that the women were most often motivated by: the need for meaningful, challenging work and independence; the opportunity to initiate their own ideas, gain a sense of accomplishment and recognition; and economic necessity. Stress factors most often cited were: fear of failure, lack of capital, regulations, and lack of credibility for females in the business world. With regard to educational background, all but one of the subjects had education beyond high school; many were education majors. All had had considerable work experience in similar businesses before starting their own businesses. The women reported that support from their families was important to them, as was assistance from business organizations and networks. They tended to be inner-directed rather than outer-directed, and were optimistic about the future.

Waddell, Frederick Thomas. "Factors Affecting Choice, Satisfaction and Success in the Female Self-Employed." Unpublished Ph.D. Dissertation, Ohio State University, 1982.

The major hypothesis for this study was that a model consisting of four variables (achievement motivation, locus of control, sex-role masculinity, and role models for ownership) would significantly discriminate between three groups of women--small business owners, managers, and secretaries. The three groups of women, apparently a non-random sample of volunteers recruited through local women's organizations, were scored on these variables throughout the use of various standardized tests and questionnaires, including the

113

Mehrabian and Bank Achievement Questionnaire, the Rotter Locus of Control Scale, and the Bem Sex Role Inventory.

It was found that these variables together could discriminate among the three occupational groups. Furthermore, business owners scored higher than secretaries in achievement motivation, locus of control internality, and sex-role masculinity, but there were no significant differences between owners and managers with respect to these variables when taken individually. Degree of job satisfaction (as measured by the Brophy Vocational Satisfaction Scale) and success in business were not significantly related to the explanatory variables taken together.

Welsch, Harold and Earl Young. "Comparative Analysis of Male and Female Entrepreneurs with Respect to Personality Characteristics, Small Business Problems, and Information Source Preferences." March 15, 1982. Mimeographed.

This paper is one of several resulting from a survey of a small sample of male and female business owners. Here, the authors attempt to distinguish significant differences between male and female entrepreneurs with respect to personality characteristics, perceptions of problems encountered, information source preferences, demographic characteristics and interest in small business seminars. This study is designed to provide an in-depth analysis of selected entrepreneurial characteristics based on statistical data in a comparative framework.

A two-tailed test was applied to test for differences between the samples of male and female entrepreneurs (see Young and Welsch, below, for description of sample). The results showed no significant differences in personality characteristics (including self-esteem and risk taking) except economic optimism. Women proved to be more optimistic than men. With respect to information sources, the data showed women to value written information sources significantly more than men. There was no significant difference with respect to preferences for other sources of information.

Women differed from men in various demographic characteristics. The women entrepreneurs surveyed were younger, had more education, less experience in the field, less business experience and lower sales volumes, but had virtually the same number of full-time employees and age of business as men entrepreneurs. The study also showed that the women were more interested in attending specialized seminars for small business.

Young, Earl C. and Harold Welsch. "Differences Between Male and Female Entrepreneurs with Respect to Personality Characteristics Relating to Information Search Behavior." 1982. Mimeographed.

In this paper a comparative analysis of male and female entrepreneurs was conducted to determine if they differed significantly with respect to the relationships between personality characteristics and information-seeking behavior. The personality dimensions of focus of control, Machiavellianism, self-esteem, risk taking, openness to innovation and rigidity were utilized. Significant differences were found between males and females. Self-esteem, risk taking and innovation were found to be the most accurate predictors for women entrepreneurs of information search behavior. The sample consisted of 140 women and 50 men entrepreneurs.

Since there is a great emphasis on networking by women in management, the authors felt that women entrepreneurs would also be very concerned with information sources. They hypothesized that personality characteristics of male and female entrepreneurs would differentially affect the entrepreneurs' information search behavior. This is an important issue because one theory (McGaffey and Christy) of entrepreneurship holds that successful entrepreneurs must be able to increase their capabilities to process data generated by the increasing complexity of their businesses as they expand.

Information search activity was research by asking those surveyed to rate the importance of different information sources (professional, personal, written, institutional, electronic) to their businesses. No weights were given to the sources; all were treated equally.

A Pearson correlation analysis was used to test the hypothesis, and the results were broken down by gender, type of information source, and personality characteristics. For women, self-esteem, risk taking and openness to innovation were the personality traits most highly correlated with an active information search pattern. No tests were made to determine whether differences in preferences for information sources might also be the result of differences in types of business, size of business, etc.

Data Sources

U.S. Dept. of Treasury, Internal Revenue Service. Statistics of Income: Sole Proprietorship Returns . Washington, D.C.: U.S. Government Printing Office, various years.

Data on the number of sole proprietorships are available for the years 1977, 1979, and 1980. The data are estimates based on a sample of unaudited returns stratified by geographic region, size of income, etc. Sole proprietorships were included in the statistics if their owners filed a Form 1040 or 1040A which included a businesses or farm schedule (C or F) or a Form 4835 (for farm rental income and expenses). Under the law, that should include anyone who had self-employment income of $400 or more. The data have several limitations, which are discussed in the introduction. For example, if ownership of a business changed during a given year, that business would be counted more than once.

U.S. Department of Commerce, Bureau of the Census. Selected Characteristics of Women-Owned Businesses, 1977. Washington, D.C.: U.S. Government Printing Office, 1980.

A survey of a sample of 25,000 women-owned businesses was conducted by the Bureau of the Census as a companion to the 1977 Census of Women-Owned Businesses. The survey revealed the following information about women business owners and their firms:

- median net income for women-owned businesses was $6,481

- 70 percent of businesses had no employees

- 80 percent of the businesses were started with $10,000 or less

- more than 60 percent were financed from the owner's savings

- the median age of owners was 52 years

- 73 percent of the owners were not married

- 90 percent of the owners were white and non-Hispanic

- 75 percent of the owners had some schooling beyond high school

- this was the first involvement in business ownership for 86 percent of the owners, but they had a median of 14.9 years' experience as paid employees and 7.4 years of managerial experience.

- 70 percent of the owners were the original founders of their businesses

- 46 percent of the businesses were located at the owner's residence.

_____. Women-Owned Businesses, 1972. Washington, D.C.: U.S. Government Printing Office, 1976.

Information is presented by industry, geographic area, employment size, receipts size, and legal form of organization. Separate information is included on minority women business owners and their firms.

The principle data source was tax returns of the Internal Revenue Sources for sole proprietorships, partnerships and small business corporations (with 10 shareholders or less), and data from the Social Security Administration. The census was conducted on the basis of firms as a whole, not individual establishments (which is often the basis for other economic censuses). It is also non-comparable with other economic censuses because of different industrial scope and no limit on receipts size for inclusion of women-owned businesses.

Summary of findings: In 1972 there were 402,025 women-owned businesses, 4.6 percent of all U.S. firms (0.3 percent of all receipts). Of the women-owned firms, 71 percent were in retail trade and selected services; only 13 percent were employer firms, but these accounted for 57 percent of total receipts; and of the employer firms, 73 percent had less than five employees.

_____. Women-Owned Businesses, 1977. Washington, D.C.: U.S. Government Printing Office, 1980.

Information included here is not directly comparable with data in the 1972 census because industrial coverage was expanded in 1977 and processing errors in 1977 caused partnerships and small corporations to be underrepresented in that year. The same data sources were utilized as in the 1972 census.

Summary of findings: In 1977 there were 701,957 women-owned firms in the United States--these represented 7.1 percent of all U.S. firms (6.6 percent in total receipts); 75 percent of the women-owned firms were in selected services and retail; those firms with paid employees represented 23.9 percent of the total, but accounted for 85 percent of gross receipts; and only 437 women-owned firms (0.3 percent of employer firms) had 100 employees or more.

U.S. Department of Labor, Bureau of Labor Statistics. Employment and Earnings. Various Issues.

This publication provides information on the number of self-employed persons, by gender, race and industry on a regular basis.

U.S. Small Business Administration. The State of Small Business: A Report to the President. Washington, D.C.: U.S. Government Printing Office, various years.

Each year The State of Small Business includes an appendix or chapter on women-owned businesses which reviews the latest sources of data, often including compilations not available elsewhere.

Financial Access for Women Business Owners

Card, Emily. Women and Mortgage Credit: An Annotated Bibliography. Washington, D.C.: U.S. Department of Housing and Urban Development, 1979. (NTIS Accession number: 82-144387).

Chapman, Jane Roberts. "Sex Discrimination in Credit: The Backlash of Economic Dependency." In Economic Independence for Women, ed. Jane Roberts Chapman. Beverly Hills, CA: Sage Publications, 1976.

This article provides excellent background on discriminatory practices that limited women's access to credit before the passage of The Equal Credit Opportunity Act (ECOA) and reviews available empirical evidence on sex discrimination in lending and women's credit worthiness. It focuses also on the relationship between women's economic status and their lack of access to credit--both consumer and commercial. The problems of women entrepreneurs are specifically addressed. The author offers insights into how current perceptions of the credit worthiness of women could have been shaped by past practices--customary and/or legal. She argues that some women's economic dependence makes them ineligible for credit in their own right, but that the mistaken presumption that all women are dependent makes lenders wary of granting credit to any woman.

Dearhammer, William G. "Equal Credit Opportunity Act/Regulation B Application to Business Credit." Journal of Commercial Bank Lending (September 1981): 2-12.

A review of ECOA and the Consumer Credit Protection Act in general with a discussion of Regulation B and how the elements of that regulation apply to business credit. Although ECOA was primarily designed to affect consumer credit (it does not specify business credit), it does not rule out application to business credit.

This article, written by a Chicago banker, takes the creditor's point of view--its main purpose is to inform creditors about the Act and Regulation B so that they can ensure their compliance. It can be, nevertheless, of interest to researchers, as it provides a concise background documentation of the issues involved in access to business credit for women and ECOA.

Farrell, Kevin. "Closing the Funding Gap." Venture 6,11 (November 1984): 72-76.

According to the author, investors are becoming more interested in women-owned businesses that are searching for venture capital. However, women may still be at a disadvantage if they do not have the corporate experience preferred by investors.

The article also discusses the growth in the number of women-owned businesses and private sector programs that have sprung up to help them, including the Resource Center for Women in California and the National Association of Bank Women's "Money and Your Business" program for women entrepreneurs.

Glassman, Cynthia A. and Peter L. Struck. "Survey of Commercial Bank Lending to Small Business." Studies of Small Business Finance. Washington, D.C.: The Interagency Task Force on Small Business Finance, 1982.

This is a report on a 1981 nationwide survey of commercial bank small business lending practices. Information was gathered through personal interviews with officers knowledgeable about small business lending at 224 sample banks. The results showed that commercial banks considered themselves to be the primary institutional sources of small business credit. The dollar volume of small business loans to total business loans ranged from 95 percent to

77 percent for banks with under $1 billion in assets (the corresponding ratio was only 13 percent for banks with over $1 billion in assets).

For the banks surveyed, average credit application approval rates during 1981 were equal for small and large businesses, at a level of 73 percent when aggregated across all banks. Credit applications for new businesses had an average approval rate of only 50 percent. The main reason given for rejecting a small business loan application was "not enough owner's equity in the business." Also cited as grounds for rejection were: poor earnings records, new firm with no established record, and slow past loan repayment. It is interesting to note that average interest rates charged to small businesses were about the same as the average rates for loans to large businesses, but the rates varied over a wider range for small business loans.

Pages 72-73, 80 and 82 of the report provide information regarding the charge-off rate (value of loans written off due to non-payment per dollar of loans outstanding) for loans to women-owned businesses relative to all small business loans from the banks surveyed. The data indicate that the charge-off rate of loans to women-owned businesses is believed to be about the same as that of all small businesses in about three-fourths of all the banks surveyed. For banks at which those charge-off rates differ, the rate for women-owned businesses as compared to that for all small business loans is lower almost three times as often as it is higher.

> JACA Corporation (Faith Ando, principal investigator). "Access to Capital and or Credit by Subcategories of Small Business." Office of Economic Research, U.S. Small Business Administration. Publication expected January 1986.

This study, the first of its kind, seeks to determine access to capital and credit by small business owners subdivided by race-by-sex. A national database was developed, and a matched sample of 400 male- and 400 female-owned businesses was selected, comparable in size and standard industrial classifacation.

This sample was then administered a questionnaire designed to discern barriers to finance, and to identify determinants of access to financial markets. The report describes the size and importance of each identified determinant to capital access for the sex-by-race subcategories of small business owners. Policy recommendations based on the findings are included.

A summary of the literature on access to business capital by women and minorities is included, and a bibliography.

> Ladd, Helen F. "Equal Credit Opportunity: Women and Mortgage Credit." American Economic Review 72, 2 (May 1982): 166-170.

The Equal Credit Opportunity Act (ECOA) was enacted in order to correct discriminatory treatment of women by the credit industry. Evidence had indicated that discrimination on the part of mortgage lenders was widespread. For example, surveys conducted in the early 1970's revealed that mortgage lenders often discounted the wife's income by 50 percent or more when evaluating applications.

This paper addresses the question of how well mortgage lenders have complied with the ECOA provisions that banned discrimination on the basis of sex and marital status. It presents the results of the author's study (with Robert Schaffer, see citation below) of lending, using mortgage applications data from New York and California. The analysis presented provides only limited evidence that lenders discriminate against female-only or certain types of male-female households. The results do indicate that lenders in some New York areas discriminate against unmarried and separated male-female households, and that lenders in New York and California treat male-only households adversely. Women may be discriminated against through lender's underappraisal of properties they purchase.

Moskowitz, Daniel B. and Irene Pave. "Battling Another Bias in Business Lending." Business Week (May 27, 1985): 68, 70.

This article describes the difficulty some women business owners face when they try to secure commercial loans. For many, the hurdles appear when they are not married, or their husbands have poor credit records or are not willing to cosign a loan application. Discrimination based on sex or marital status in granting credit was prohibited by the Equal Credit Opportunity Act. However, the regulation for implementing the Act exempted business loans from certain practices banks were required to follow in handling consumer credit applications. A bill which has been introduced in Congress would extend the regulation to cover commercial as well as personal loans. If the bill becomes law, banks would then be unable to ask business borrowers about their marital status and would be required to give written notice of the reasons for rejecting a loan application.

O'Connor, W. J., Jr. "The Equal Credit Opportunity Act and Business Credit--Some Problems Considered." Journal of Commercial Bank Lending 61 (January 1979): 20-36.

The article reviews legislative action and litigation associated with ECOA, which was passed in 1975 and amended and expanded in 1977. Particular attention is focused on Regulation B, the regulation adopted by the Federal Reserve to implement ECOA.

The Act prohibited discrimination in business and consumer credit on the basis of sex, marital status, race, color, religion, national origin, age, receipt of income from public assistance programs, and the exercise of any rights under the Consumer Credit Protection Act. Regulation B exempted business credit from the notification, furnishing of information/reasons for refusal and record retention provisions that apply to consumer credit. An amendment was proposed in 1978 that would eliminate the business credit exemptions on direct loans up to $100,000. This article identifies and considers special problems for business creditors raised by Regulation B, including: effects tests, determining what constitutes an application, co-signers, and corporate applicants.

Peterson, Richard L. "An Investigation of Sex Discrimination in Commercial Banks' Direct Consumer Lending." Bell Journal of Economics 12 (Autumn 1981): 547-561.

This article proposes a model of prejudicial discrimination in credit markets. Data on 30,000 commercial bank consumer loans in five categories were used to test the model. The data were collected by the Federal Reserve System from 30 sample banks in five regions during the period 1966-1971. Information was provided on 100 percent of all charged-off loans (loans written off due to non-payment) and 10 percent of paid-off and new loans. The researcher tested for sex-related differences in: the ratio of losses to total value of loans, the probability of loss, and interest rates charged.

No systematic pattern of prejudicial sex discrimination was found. The author concluded that banks as a whole had behaved as profit-maximizers, making loans on equivalent terms to equally risky customers, regardless of sex.

However, a serious flaw in the design of this study is its exclusive focus on loans granted, not on all applications (including rejections). Also not considered were informal (i.e., verbal) applications and bank requirements for cosigners (anecdotal evidence suggests that married women were often required to have their spouse cosign for commercial bank loans).

Reno, Barbara Morrison, ed. Credit and Women's Economic Development. Washington, D.C.: World Council of Credit Unions, Inc., September 1981.

The World Council of Credit Unions, in collaboration with the Chase Manhattan Bank, organized a program for the United Nations Mid-Decade Forum of the International Decade for Women. The program was entitled, "Women Entrepreneurs: Access to Capital and Credit." Program panelists included women entrepreneurs and representatives of financial and other institutions involved in making loans for productive purposes.

The report on the conference was written primarily for policy makers and program designers concerned with income-generating projects that involve credit and women. The report is divided into three parts. Part I provides a brief discussion of income generation, entrepreneurship and credit access to women. Part II consists of edited presentations and profiles of the panelists. In Part III observations of the panelists are summarized in three categories: credit access, enterprise development, and loan program design.

Schaffer, Robert and Helen F. Ladd. <u>Equal Credit Opportunity: Accessibility to Mortgage Funds by Women and by Minorities: Final Technical Report</u>. Joint Center for Urban Studies of the Massachusetts Institute of Technology and Harvard University. Washington, D.C.: U.S. Government Printing Office, 1980.

A two-volume report on a study conducted as part of the research component of the Women and Mortgage Credit Project at the U.S. Department of Housing and Urban Development. It is based on an examination of data on rejected and accepted mortgage applications for California and New York.

The study did not reveal whether or not discrimination was taking place at the pre-application stage--i.e., if lenders discouraged women and minorities from applying. But the study revealed little evidence of discrimination against women in the mortgage market or of discounting of women's income. It did show widespread discrimination against minorities and some evidence of discrimination against "male-only" households.

U.S. Treasury Department Study Team. <u>Credit and Capital Formation: A Report to the President's Interagency Task Force on Women Business Owners</u>. Washington, D.C.: Department of Treasury, 1978.

This is the only study of its kind and, until recently (see JACA entry), nearly the only piece of serious research to address the subject of commercial credit for women. The document reviews the credit and capital access problems small business owners face with an overall emphasis on the woman business owner and how she is affected by these problems. It presents and analyzes the results of a survey of 3,000 women business owners conducted by the President's Task Force on Women Business Owners, roundtable discussions with bankers and entrepreneurs held in six major U.S. cities, and interviews with bank loan officers.

The findings of the Study Team were inconclusive. Little or no direct evidence was found to support the notion that women have unique problems in obtaining business credit, all other considerations being equal. In fact, the women surveyed appear to have relatively good access to commercial bank credit (relying on loans for start-up financing in 21.5 percent of the cases), although very few (only 0.5 percent) had access to venture capital for initial financing. The study suffers from the lack of a sample of male business owners for comparison. In addition, the results reported are based on subjective responses of the women business owners to questions about credit, etc., not on actual applications.

The report is divided into four parts: financial aspects of pre-entry to business ownership and actual market entry, capital formation (including access to venture capital), credit, and taxation issues. Each of the sections discusses the financial needs and requirements of women business owners, barriers to meeting those needs, existing programs and legislation, and recommendations for action.

Government Programs for Women Business Owners

Review of Government Programs

"All the President's Women: Update on Progress of Interagency Committee on Women's Business Enterprise." Enterprising Women 1 (1979): 6-7.

This brief article reports on the activities and the personnel involved in the work of the Interagency Committee on Women's Business Enterprise, which was formed to implement the recommendations of the President's Task Force on Women Business Owners. Representatives from 30 federal agencies, departments and the White House were named to the Committee following the signing of Executive Order 12138 in May 1979. The article comments on Small Business Administration programs, including targeting of direct loans to women-owned businesses and efforts to increase the number of women-owned firms in the SBA's Procurement Automated Source System (PASS).

Berry, M.C. "Targeting More Aid to Women Entrepreneurs." Venture 2 (May 1980): 49-52.

Berry points out that there is an increasing awareness on the part of the government of the special financing problems that women face. Some of these problems are poor credit ratings, social biases, and unequal opportunity to secure government contracts. The article reviews affirmative action policies adopted by government agencies to help women in business.

Boone, Young & Associates. "Improving Contracting Opportunities for Women's Business Enterprises in the City of Pittsburgh." November 1985. (Available from Mayor's Task Force on Women in Renaissance II, 518 City-County Bldg., Pittsburgh, PA 15219.)

Report includes a description of the city's existing procedures (including goal-setting processes) and legislation, a summary and analysis of interviews conducted with city personnel and women business owners, a summary of techniques used by comparable municipalities, and a historical overview of the experience of women business owners in the United States. Recommendations are made in the area of legislation, administrative program support and methodology for establishment of goals.

"Businesswomen Get A Champion At SBA." Nation's Business 65 (December 1977): 34-36

A profile of Patricia Cloherty, a former deputy administrator of the Small Business Administration, describes her efforts on behalf of women business owners. Before taking a job at SBA, Ms. Cloherty was a partner in a New York venture capital firm. The article describes efforts made to offer more management assistance, financial assistance, advocacy, and assistance in securing federal contracts for women business owners as part of President Carter's Women's Business Ownership Campaign, begun in August 1977.

According to Cloherty, SBA assistance to women started by using existing programs, together with seminars for prospective women business owners, individual counseling by Service Corps of Retired Executives (SCORE) volunteers and enhanced SBA outreach to women. Efforts were also to be made to promote and hire more women within SBA.

Ms. Cloherty noted that in her experience with Alan Patricof Associates, the few women-owned businesses that sought venture capital from the firm were generally considered unattractive to outside investors looking for long-term capital gains. She remarked that the SBA, on the other hand, "doesn't invest for capital gains, but for business development purposes."

Gordon, Alice K, Emily Lusker and Meredith Webb Women-Owned Small Business: Winning in the Federal Marketplace 3 vols. Washington, D.C.: CRC Education and Human Development, Inc., 1981.

This study sought to identify women-owned businesses that had been successful in federal procurement, and to determine what distinguished them from other women-owned firms not yet successful in marketing to the government and those that had not attempted to participate in federal contracting. The purpose of the study was to identify factors that contributed to success in order to help other women-owned businesses that are interested in Federal procurement.

Volume I of the three-volume study describes the characteristics which distinguish winners from bidders and bidders from non-bidders. In addition, recommendations for a federal strategy based on this information are presented.

One thousand women business owners were selected for the survey from those listed in the Procurement Automated Source System (PASS). Of the 549 responding, 215 were contract winners, 132 unsuccessful bidders and 202 non-bidders. The authors point out that the sample was probably biased because firms registering for PASS could be assumed to have an interest in selling to the Federal Government. No attempt was made to compare women- and men-owned firms.

The authors concluded that:

- women-owned businesses in the sample tended to be larger and more formally organized than women-owned businesses in general

- within the sample, bidders tended to be owners of larger, better organized, more formally structured businesses

- there were strong differences in the methods of marketing to the Federal Government between winners on the one hand and non-winners/non-bidders on the other hand

- the attitude of winners was more positive--winners exhibited active learning behavior, they conducted a more active search for information and contacts and they learned how to win

- the Federal Government was generally seen as a difficult client by those surveyed, one that treats potential suppliers poorly.

Volume II of the study describes in detail the characteristics of the survey respondents that have been successful in obtaining government contracts. The 40 businesses profiled sold 35 different products and services to various federal agencies and departments. The firms varied in size and number of years in operation. The average sales volume was $800,000 to $900,000 per year, but that figure varied widely across firms. Federal sales represented from 1 percent to 100 percent of total sales, with a median of 30 percent.

The firms had obtained their contracts primarily through standard competitive bidding. Although the 40 owners considered themselves knowledgeable about the procurement process used by the government, over half claimed not to have a "well-defined sales strategy." They stressed persistence, hard work, playing fair, knowing the field, taking risks, and being aggressive more than marketing plans, targets and goals, return on investment, or firmly projected capture rates. As a whole they seemed to choose as their major marketing strategy a high level of reliance on personal contacts on a one-to-one basis. The owners generally attributed their problems to those of all small businesses, rather than to their gender.

Volume III describes the technical details of how the study was conducted, including how the sample was selected, how the data were collected, information about response rates, what specific analysis techniques were employed, and the significance of test results for each hypothesis.

"Federal Nurturing for Female Entrepreneurs." Nation's Business 67 (August 1979): 77-78.

This article focuses on Executive Order 12138, which established a women's business enterprise policy in 1979. It also describes the programs designed to help women business owners, implemented by various federal government agencies. Some of the programs discussed include:

- a $50 million Small Business Administration experimental program to provide direct loans under $20,000 to women-owned businesses (the "Mini-Loan Program)

- SBA efforts to add 15,000 women-owned businesses to PASS by the end of FY 1980

- an Office of Federal Procurement Policy effort to double the amount of federal prime contracts to women-owned businesses to $150 million in FY 1980 and to redouble that amount in FY 1981

- establishment of a data base on female entrepreneurs that do business with the government and encouragement of subcontracting to women-owned businesses

- development of new programs for elementary and secondary schools to promote entrepreneurship as a career option for women

O'Brien, P. "Uncle Is Listening, But Will He Hear?" Inc. 2 (January 1980): 68-73.

The author discusses the issues facing delegates to the January 1980 White House Conference on Small Business. Fifty-seven pre-conference meetings were held with approximately 30,000 participants. The 1,400 delegates elected to the conference were to be joined by 700 other delegates appointed by state governments and members of Congress, and 11 commissioners named by the President to organize the conference and to draft the final report. Minorities and women were expected to be well-represented.

The main issues raised with respect to women in business were: extension of the Equal Credit Opportunity Act to cover commercial credit; creation of an office of women's business enterprise at the Small Business Administration at the level of Associate Administrator; subcontracting set-asides for women-owned businesses by government prime contractors; targeting 10 percent of SBA guaranteed loans to women-owned businesses; and insuring that Small Business Development Centers (SDBC's) design programs that are relevant and accessible to women.

Ann Parker Maust and Mary Greiner. "An Analysis of Smaller Firm Participation." Washington, D.C.: Office of Economic Research, U.S. Small Business Administration, 1983.

This report provides federal procurement information for the first time, by employment, size of firm, minority status, and sex. Fiscal Year 1981 was the only year studied because it was the most recent year for which complete Federal Procurement Data Center data were available at the time the study was initiated.

Key findings related to women as federal contractors were as follows:

- 80 percent of all "small" federal contractors had less than 100 employees; 89 percent of women contractors fell in this category

- 55 percent of the women "small" contractors had fewer than 20 employees

- the dollar amount to women "small" contractors with fewer than 20 employees (contracts of more than $10,000) was less than .06 percent ($68 million)

- only 34 of 54 agencies reported any awards to women at all. Of these, only three awarded more than 17 percent of their contracts over $10,000 to women (Consumer Product Safety Commission, Federal Communications Commission and the U.S. Small Business Administration)

- very small (fewer than 20 employees) women-owned firms received less per employee in contracts than this size firm generally or than minority-owned firms of this size (women: $13,900 per employee; very small firms in general: $19,300 per employee; and minorities: $30,900).

SMS Associates. A Small Business Guide: A Directory of Federal Government Business Assistance Programs for Women Business Owners. Washington, D.C.: U.S. Department of Commerce, 1980.

Prepared for the Economic Development Administration, U.S. Department of Commerce. (An updated version will be released by the Small Business Administration in the near future.)

U.S. Commission on Civil Rights. Minorities and Women as Government Contractors. Washington, D.C.: U.S. Civil Rights Commission, 1975, updated 1977.

This report analyzes the extent to which minorities and women share in the billions of dollars of federal, state and local government contracts awarded annually. It also focuses on the problems encountered by minority and women-owned firms seeking government contracts, the opportunities provided to minority firms through special contracting programs, and the extent to which non-minority women are entitled to participate in these programs.

Data were gathered through questionnaires sent to federal agencies, and state and local programs. Investigations revealed that minority and women-owned firms encountered formidable problems in obtaining timely information on federal, state and local contracting opportunities, and the working capital necessary for effective marketing and bidding. They also face skepticism regarding their ability to perform adequately on government contracts. Evidence indicated that the women-owned firms participate even less than minority-owned firms in all levels of government procurement.

The Commission found that special federal programs designed to assist minority-owned firms had experienced limited success in increasing the number and dollar value of contracts awarded to those firms. But the programs had been successful in assisting minority-owned firms with working capital problems and obtaining timely information on government contracting opportunities.

The report includes recommendations on improving access to federal procurement for women and minorities. The need for firmly established goals for contracting to target groups and better data on procurement are highlighted. Extensive breakdown of available data is provided in tables.

U.S. Department of Commerce. The Guide to the U.S. Department of Commerce for Women Business Owners. Washington, D.C.: U.S. Government Printing Office, 1980.

This booklet identifies Department of Commerce programs that can help women business owners. The purpose of each agency is stated, followed by a description of applicable programs available to the woman entrepreneur.

U.S. General Accounting Office. Report to the Administrator, Small Business Administration: Need to Determine Whether Existing Programs Can Meet the Needs of Women Entrepreneurs. Washington, D.C.: General Accounting Office, 1981.

In its report, the General Accounting Office contended that the SBA and the Interagency Committee on Women's Business Enterprise had not given enough attention to using existing SBA and other federal resources to meet the needs of women entrepreneurs, focusing instead on designing new programs.

The GAO argued that many of the difficulties women experience in establishing a business, which were cited by women business owners and women's organizations in the reports and congressional testimony of the mid 1970's, were problems commonly faced by all small businesses. Those problems include lack of capital, insufficient management and technical skills, and difficulties with product marketability. However, the authors of the GAO report agreed that social prejudices, such as a credibility gap with contractors and bankers, intensify those problems for women business owners.

The report summarized the findings of a GAO review of federal initiatives undertaken in the first year following issuance of Executive Order 12138. The annual reports of the 17 federal agencies represented on the Interagency Committee on Women's Business Enterprise were reviewed. The GAO concluded that initiatives designed to increase procurement opportunities for women-owned businesses were the primary focus of federal agency efforts in FY 1980. It was argued that a lack of operating procedures was a major problem for the Women's Business Enterprise Division of the SBA and that the Interagency Committee had not provided adequate guidance to federal agencies for administering Executive Order 12138.

The report also emphasized the importance of evaluating existing federal programs and resources to determine whether they adequately address the needs of women entrepreneurs.

U.S. Interagency Committee on Women's Business Enterprise. Women Business Owners: Selling to the Federal Government. Washington, D.C.: U.S. Small Business Administration, 1984.

This practical guide directed at women business owners provides information on marketing goods and services to the Federal Government. The booklet discusses government procurement mechanisms and procedures, bidding on government contracts, subcontracting, standard forms required by the government, and assistance provided by different agencies. It also includes a bibliography of government publications that provide further information and guidelines on selling to particular departments or agencies.

White House Conference on Small Business. America's Small Business Economy: Agenda for Action. Washington, D.C.: U.S. Government Printing Office, 1980.

This document presents the findings and recommendations of the White House Conference on Small Business, held in January 1980, and attended by 1,682 delegates and 3,600 other participants from around the country. Recommendations 36-40 apply directly to women-owned businesses. These are:

(No. 36)   recommends extension of record keeping provisions of the Equal Credit Opportunity Act to commercial credit and the establishment of targets for loans to women-owned and minority-owned businesses as one criterion for SBA recertification of banks participating in the certified lenders program

(No. 37)   urges establishment of mandatory goals for federal procurement--50 percent of the total for small business specifically, 10 percent for women-owned businesses, 15 percent for minority-owned businesses and 25 percent for other small businesses

(No. 38)   recommends that SBA identify and evaluate the effectiveness of public and private management training programs for meeting the needs of women business owners

(No. 39)   proposes that Federal Government employees' performance be evaluated in part on the basis of their efforts on behalf of women and minorities

(No. 40)   states that SBA should establish a bonding program to permit the waiver of bonding requirements for federal contractors who are small business owners.

Congressional Hearings

U. S. Congress. Joint Economic Committee. Conference on Measuring Progress in Participation by Minority and Female Contractors in Federal Procurement: Report of the Joint Economic Committee. 1978.

This report on a conference held September 23, 1977, includes statements and testimony by government officials, members of Congress, and representatives of women and minority business owners. Discussion focuses on the need to have adequate data on procurement by women-owned businesses and minority businesses in order to monitor access to government procurement money, to ensure it is available on a non-discriminatory basis, and to evaluate progress being made toward achieving the overall goal of business development for women and minorities.

U.S. Congress. House. Committee on Small Business. Subcommittee on General Oversight and Minority Enterprise. Women in Business: Hearings before the Subcommittee on Minority Enterprise and General Oversight of the Committee on Small Business. 95th Congress, 1st session, 1977.

Most of the testimony presented at this hearing by advocates for women's business ownership focused on the inferior economic status of women as well as social biases against women business owners. The lack of equal opportunities for women to enter business was stressed--especially with respect to lack of training and finance. There was also an emphasis on the U.S. Small Business Administration's handling of women business owners, including discussion of whether SBA's programs were meeting the needs of women business owners and whether these owners were being treated fairly by the SBA. The use of federal procurement as a tool for general business development for women and minority-owned businesses was another major topic.

Supporting documents included in the record include a detailed position paper on the participation of women-owned firms in federal procurement, prepared by Marilyn Andrulis, president of Andrulis Research Corporation, and a pamphlet, "The Facts About Women as Users of SBA Services in FY's 1974, 1975 and 1976." The latter provides information on loans to women-owned businesses by category of loan, by industry, and by race, as well as information on the number of women using SBA management assistance services.

The hearing record includes testimony and statements by: Dr. Tena Cummings, Executive Director, National Federation of Business and Professional Women's Clubs, Inc.; Frankie M. Freeman, Commissioner, U.S. Civil Rights Commission; Inez Kaiser, President, National Association of Minority Women in Business; Juanita Kreps, Secretary of Commerce; Donna O'Bannon, President, National Association of Women Business Owners; Susan Hager, President, Hager-Sharp Associates, Inc.; Lori Simmons, Vice President, WLS Design Associates, Ltd.; and Vernon Weaver, Administrator, U.S. Small Business Administration.

_____. Women in Business: A Report. 95th Congress, 1st session, 1977. H. Rept. 95-604.

This report summarizes testimony received during hearings held April 5, May 23, and June 7, 1977 [see entry above]. The hearings were held to review the status of women in business, and to assess Federal efforts to promote the economic development of female entrepreneurs. The report includes subcommittee conclusions and recommendations, and various tables.

_____. Women in Business: Hearing before the Subcommittee on General Oversight and Minority Enterprise of the Committee on Small Business. 96th Congress, 2d session, 1980.

This document contains transcripts of testimony and statements of Rilla Woods, Chairperson, Interagency Committee on Women's Business Enterprise;

Marcia Bystrom, Assistant Administrator, U.S. Small Business Administration, Office of Women's Business Enterprise; Karen H. Williams, Administrator, Office of Federal Procurement Policy; Marge Rossman, President, National Association of Women Business Owners; Marilyn Andrulis, President of the National Association of Women Government Contractors; and Beatrice Fitzpatrick, American Woman's Economic Development Corporation; as well as several members of Congress.

The main points of discussion centered on policy isses related to ensuring fair access to procurement for women-owned businesses, access to credit and capital for women-owned businesses, and the provisions of Executive Order 12138. Newspaper and magazine articles on women-owned businesses are included in the record.

> U.S. Congress. Senate. Select Committee on Small Business. Women-in-Business Programs in the Federal Government: Hearing before the Select Committee on Small Business. 96th Congress, 2d session, 1980.

Testimony and statements at this hearing focused on Small Business Administration programs specifically designed for women and those that benefit women as well as men. The testimony provides an overview of women's experiences in establishing and operating businesses, including special problems of black women business owners. Discussion centered on efforts to bring more women-owned businesses onto the Procurement Automated Source System (PASS), management assistance, direct loans to women-owned businesses (including the SBA pilot mini-loan program), the American Woman's Economic Development Corporation (AWED), and the possibilities of including women-owned businesses in Public Law 95-507 and the 8(a) subcontracting program.

Testimony was given by: William Mauk, Deputy Administrator of the SBA; Thelma Moss, Acting Chair, Coalition of Women in National and International Business; Marilyn Andrulis, National Association of Women Federal Contractors; Beatrice Fitzpatrick, Chief Executive Officer of AWED; Donna Shalala, Chair, Business Development Subcommittee, Interagency Committee on Women's Business Enterprise; Marilyn French-Hubbard, President, National Association of Black Women Entrepreneurs; Marlene Johnson, Treasurer, National Association of Women Business Owners; Virginia Littlejohn, President, American Independent Women Business Owners.

> _____. The Effects of Government Regulations on Small Business and the Problems of Women and Minorities in Small Business in the Southwestern United States. 94th Congress, 2d session. 1976.

Testimony by Senators and Representatives of the U.S. Congress and representatives of the business community in the Southwestern United States focuses on government policy, SBA activities and the problems small businesses (particularly women and minority-owned) face as a result of government regulations.

_____. Associate Administrator for Women's Business Enterprise within the Small Business Administration: Report to Accompany S. 1526. 95th Congress, 1st session, 1977. S. Report 95-406.

This 4-page report recommends passage of S. 1526, to amend the Small Business Act in order to establish the position of SBA Associate Administrator for Women's Business Enterprise.

_____. Establish an Associate Administrator at SBA for Women's Business Enterprise: Hearing on S.1526. 95th Congress, 1st session, 1977.

This document provides a brief compilation of testimony on the need to establish the position of Associate Administrator for Women's Business Enterprise at the Small Business Administration in order to ensure that SBA more adequately meets the needs of women in business. Included are testimony and statements by members of Congress; Eve Grover, Vice President, Women's Headquarters, State National Bank of Maryland; Meredith Homet, Committee to Organize the Women's National Bank; Donna O'Bannon, President, National Association of Women Business Owners; Professor Bobbye Persing, Central State University, Business Department; and Vernon Weaver, Administrator, U.S. Small Business Administration.

_____. Women and the Small Business Administration: Hearing before the Select Committee on Small Business. 94th Congress, 2d session, 1976.

During this hearing discussion centered on the representation of women in the 8(a) program, SBA assistance to women business owners, access to credit for women business owners, the lack of information on women-owned businesses and their problems and the need to improve that information. Senators John Glenn and William Brock made opening remarks. Testimony was given by: Inez Austin, Second Vice President, National Association of Women Business Owners; Denise Cavanaugh, Finance Officer, National Association of Women Business Owners, and partner, Cook/Cavanaugh Associates; Jane R. Chapman, Co-Director, Center for Women's Policy Studies; Eve Grover, State National Bank of Maryland; Susan Hager, President, National Association of Women Business Owners; Louis Laun, Deputy Administrator, SBA; and Dorothy Rivers, Chairperson, National Women's Division, Chicago Economic Development Corporation.

_____. Women Entrepreneurs: Their Success and Problems. Hearing before the Committee on Small Business. 98th Congress, 2nd session, 1984.

A congressional hearing called in Oregon to gather information and testimony on women business owners and any unusual problems they might encounter. Included is testimony from Big Ben Shopper, Inc., United States Business and Professional Women (BPW/USA); Rural Small Business Programs, Lane Community College; Master-Engineering, Ltd.; Four Seasons Advertising Design; Riverside

Equipment Service; Mary Seeman Interior Designs; Women Entrepreneurs of Oregon; Jean Tate Real Estate; and the National Association of Bank Women (NABW).

Education and Training for Women Business Owners

American Woman's Economic Development Corporation, Helping Women Learn to Mind Their Own Business. Economic Development Administration, U.S. Department of Commerce, 1979. (NTIS Accession No.: PB-299 322/8SL.)

This report documents the history of the American Woman's Economic Development Corporation (AWED). The program was created in 1976 with a $124,531 grant from the Department of Commerce's Economic Development Administration for the purpose of developing a model entrepreneurial assistance program for women which was to be replicated in cities across the country.

AWED's program as described herein includes: screening interviews, management training, business plan preparation, personal counseling, a network of women business owners to share advice and experiences, and an end-of-year interview to assess progress.

This report describes the development and implementation of AWED, as well as future plans. It also discusses the strengths and needs of women entrepreneurs and provides 10 case studies of AWED clients.

Arthur D. Little, Inc. The American Woman's Economic Development Corporation: An Evaluation. Washington, D.C.: Office of Technical Assistance, Economic Development Administration, U.S. Department of Commerce, 1980. (NTIS Accession No.: PB81-21857.)

This report discusses the American Woman's Economic Development Corporation (AWED), a model entrepreneurial assistance program for women located in New York City, initially funded by the Economic Development Administration's Office of Technical Assistance. Covered are AWED's development and operations, program impact, and recommendations for future program activities and funding strategies.

The report found that in 1979 AWED clients owned 187 businesses with 699 full-time and 647 part-time employees. The authors assert that AWED clients were contributing to employment growth and increased economic activity, but that it was not possible to tell if this strong economic activity was the result of AWED training. The estimated cost per client assisted over one full year is $2,700.

The report pointed out that AWED had developed a significant pool of resources for women business owners and maintained high visibility in New York and nationally. Since AWED built on resources readily available in most cities, the authors believe the program has potential for replication. They recommend improvements in management and organization at AWED, diversification of AWED's funding base, and the development of formal planning activity.

Bassi, Robert A. "A Credit to Banking." NABW (National Association of Bank Women) Journal (July/August 1981).

NABW's comprehensive program, "Business Financing: Preparing the Woman Entrepreneur," which was designed to assist the woman entrepreneur to understand financial alternatives that can enable her to meet her business goals is discussed. Through a workshop format, women business owners learn to assess their firms' financial situation, prepare loan requests, and negotiate loans. Unique to this particular program is the inclusion of bankers as session leaders and participants. The workshop is designed to encourage interaction between bankers and women entrepreneurs in the workshop setting to eliminate misunderstandings about the loan process.

Computer Systems Service Bureau, Inc. in Conjunction with Market Analysis System, Inc. Evaluation of the Women's Business Ownership Conferences '84, Final Report. November 1985. Available from Office of Women's Business Ownership, U.S. Small Business Administration, Washington, D.C. 20416. Contract #8501-WBED-84.

This report compiles information from 5,299 valid responses to a survey distributed at conferences for women business owners conducted from October 1983 through November 1984. The conferences were held in 21 cities throughout the United States and attended by 16,400 present and potential women business owners. Emphasis at the conferences was on building business management skills. The response rate to the survey overall was over 30 percent. Analysis of the responses yielded the following findings, among others:

- a majority of conference attendees were business owners, primarily sole proprietors in service businesses

- a majority had fewer than three full-time employees and had been in business seven years or less

- racial composition of the attendees generally tracked the proportion of women in a given racial category in the population of the SMSAs where the conferences were held.

- few had previous training in small business, and very few had been exposed to SBA-sponsored seminars

- attendees came to the conferences primarily because they wanted more information in financial management and cash flow analysis techniques. They were satisfied with the information provided, and intended to develop a business plan, conduct a cash flow analysis and attend more training events, especially on topics related to marketing and sales.

Individual National Initiative Conference evaluation reports are also available for: Atlanta, Boston, Cleveland, Dallas, Des Moines, Hartford, Houston, Indianapolis, Kansas City, Los Angeles, Minneapolis, Nashville, New Jersey, New York, Orlando, Philadelphia, Pittsburgh, Oakland, San Diego, San Francisco, and Washington, D.C.

Diffley, Judy High. "A Study of Women Business Owners and the Importance of Selected Entrepreneurial Competencies Related to Educational Programs." Ph.D. Dissertation, University of Oklahoma, 1982.

The subjects of this study were 106 self-employed women in Kansas service and retail industries. A sample of 126 (of which 106 responded) was drawn from various Kansas business directories. Among those who responded, 70 percent were married, 55 percent were an only child or the eldest, nearly 80 percent had attended college, and 48 percent had been in business for more than five years. One-third of the businesses were corporations, and almost one-half were sole proprietorships. The women surveyed had obtained business financing largely from individual savings (48.1 percent), family and friends (12.3 percent), and commercial banks (24.5 percent). Only 30 percent of those in the sample had a pre-tax net income from their businesses of $25,000 or more in 1980.

The women surveyed indicated that the three most important competencies were knowledge of customers' needs, the ability to use oral and written communication skills, and a basic familiarity with the business or industry they entered. Retail business owners indicated a greater desire for education about the entrepreneurial competencies than did service business owners, while the latter actually had a higher attendance record at entrepreneurial education sessions.

Eliason, C. Final Report: Women Business Owners Orientation Program. Washington, D.C.: Center for Women's Opportunities, American Association of Community and Junior Colleges, 1980.

The report provides an extensive background discussion of gender issues related to small business ownership, focusing particularly on the relationship between education and women's enterprise development and the role of community colleges in promoting vocational education for women business owners. It also reviews theories of entrepreneurship and sex-socialization.

The document reports on an SBA-funded project of the American Association of Community and Junior Colleges, which was designed to develop, field test and evaluate a counseling model and 45-hour competency-based curriculum package of credit and non-credit programs targeted at women who wished to buy, start or expand a small business. The field test training was completed by 370 people at 10 different locations across the country. A follow-up survey showed that 70 percent had successfully launched their business plans. The program was expected to be operating in over 300 locations by June 1981.

_____. Women Business Owners Orientation Program Guide. Washington, D.C.: Center for Women's Opportunities, American Association of Community and Junior Colleges, 1979.

Kent, Calvin A. "Entrepreneurship Education for Women: A Research Review and Agenda." Paper presented at the Joint Council on Economic Education Conference, Kansas City, MO, October 1982.

In this paper, the author describes three levels of entrepreneurship education--awareness (understanding that entrepreneurship could be a viable career option); motivation (the process of commitment to the idea of business ownership); and actualization (the planning and implementation of a business). Of these, the author cites awareness as a particular problem for women because sex stereotyping steers them away from non-traditional careers at an early age. Sex stereotyping in school tends to be a factor inhibiting women from acquiring the insights, motivation and skills necessary to become entrepreneurs.

This paper reviews literature on women business owners, characteristics of entrepreneurs, and entrepreneurship education. The author notes that no specific studies have been done to determine if training needs of women entrepreneurs are different from those of men and whether specific curricula developed with a female perspective would be useful.

He recommends:

● continued research to determine the unique needs of women business owners and appropriate educational systems to meet those needs

● evaluation of current programs to determine which are most appropriate to women business owners

● development of materials to increase awareness of female school children about entrepreneurship as a career option

● enforcement of legislation designed to reduce sex bias and stereotyping in schools

● development of materials that portray the role and importance of women business owners and

● strengthening of entrepreneurship education programs in general.

McNamara, Patricia P. "Business Ownership: A New Career Option for Women." New Directions for Education, Work and Careers 8 (1979): 71-82.

The author argues that in some respects, the situation of women vis-a-vis business ownership is similar to that of women seeking access to other "non-traditional" careers such as high-level corporate management, university administration, and the professions of engineering, law and medicine. However, women business owners differ in that they are seeking to establish an independent operation. The article also stresses the "economic marginality" of women-owned businesses, pointing out that women-owned businesses are concentrated in labor-intensive industries that require low capitalization and tend to show a lower return on investment.

The article provides background information on women business owners. It summarizes the results of a survey conducted by the California Women Entrepreneurs Project, compares them to the American Management Association survey and the President's Task Force on women business owners' survey, and describes the educational curriculum developed by the California Project.

The author identifies the major barriers to women's business ownership as:

- capital--lack of personal resources, undercapitalization of business, lack of equity in business, lack of access to credit

- negative attitudes of society (including clients and colleagues) toward women in non-traditional fields

- lack of business skills, due to socialization and education

- lack of supportive networks.

The author concludes that women business owners are satisfied with their chosen entrepreneurial careers and find business ownership exciting and rewarding. Suggestions are offered on how educational institutions could encourage women entrepreneurs and could contribute to women's preparation for business ownership.

National Association of Women Business Owners. Educational Needs of Women in Business. Washington, D.C.: Women's Education Equity Act Program, U.S. Department of Education, 1980.

A report on a November 1979 conference held by the National Association of Women Business Owners under a grant from the Women's Educational Equity Act Program, U.S. Department of Education. The goals of the conference were to devise means of assisting the Department of Education in implementing provisions of Executive Order 12138 (which created a national policy on women's business enterprise) and to find ways in which WEEA could be most responsive to women entrepreneurs. The report summarizes the conference proceedings and the recommendations for specific programs suggested by participants.

Participants identified educational needs of women business owners and made recommendations in six major areas: psychological support, educational and family systems, technical know-how, capitalization, research, and regulations. Suggestions for educational programs included: internship programs for young women and men with women-owned businesses, outreach and information dissemination on women-owned businesses for college-level business administration programs, apprenticeship programs for women in non-traditional jobs and non-traditional businesses, summer institutes, and resource materials for women business owners describing government programs.

Program presentations were made by Beatrice Fitzpatrick of the American Woman's Economic Development Corporation, Carol Eliason of the American Association of Community and Junior Colleges, and Marythea Grebner of the Southern Oregon State College Business Management Training for Rural Women program.

Office of Women's Business Ownership. Surviving Business Crises, (Training Materials). Washington, D.C.: U.S. Small Business Administration, 1983.

The training materials for Surviving Business Crises which were the final product of a 6-month pilot in 1982-83 are available for review through District and Regional Offices of the U.S. Small Business Administration. The materials include leader and participant manuals, slides, and a series of videotapes dramatizing critical events in a financial crisis faced by a fictional woman-owned retail clothing store.

Office of Women's Business Ownership. Surviving Business Crises: Final Report. Washington, D.C.: U.S. Small Business Administration, 1983. Unpublished file copy.

This report documents the development of a pilot training program in which six SBA District Offices designed and conducted specialized training programs aimed at small women-owned businesses in the first three years of existence. The project produced a six-session course emphasizing financial management skills, and a training package which is available nationwide through local SBA offices.

Solomon, George. National Women's Pre-Business Workshop Evaluation Study. Washington, D.C.: U.S. Small Business Administration, 1979.

As part of the SBA's "National Women's Business Ownership Campaign" a series of one-day Pre-Business Workshops for women were presented through SBA field offices between September 1977 and May 1978. Topics addressed included: forms of business organization, record keeping, financial factors, marketing and promotion, business regulation and taxes, and sources of capital.

A survey of participants, designed to collect information on participants and to evaluate the program, yielded 3,206 useable questionnaires. Most of the women participating were between the ages of 22 and 51. Of the women surveyed, 15 percent were from minority groups, 61 percent were married, 79 percent had at least some college, and 61 percent had no prior business management training. Most of the women (90 percent) were interested in starting a business in retail or services. None were currently in business.

The response to the workshops was positive: 80 percent rated the subject coverage and information presentation in the workshops good to excellent; 90

percent believed the workshops had been beneficial to them and an equal percentage thought the workshops had satisfied their needs. Most of those surveyed, 90 percent, indicated a desire for additional training.

Based on these and other findings, the author of the study concluded that the workshops were successful and that the results indicated they should be extended and offered on a larger scale basis.

The usefulness of this study could have been greatly enhanced by a follow-up survey of the participants to determine how many actually went into business and how useful they found the course in terms of their day-to-day operational needs. It is still, nevertheless, one of the few pieces of systematic research on the effectiveness of an SBA program in meeting the needs of women business owners.

Verble, Sedelta D. and Frances Walton. Ohoyo Training Manual. Leadership: Self-Help American Indian-Alaska Native Women. Wichita Falls, TX: Ohoyo Resource Center, 1983. ERIC Document # E0243638.

A training manual designed specifically to provide self-help for American Indian and Alaska Native women in six areas of leadership development. The manual focuses on theories and development of leadership skills, the vulnerability of Indian women to poverty, non-traditional careers for Indian women, entrepreneurship, politics, and tribal sovereignty issues. An annotated bibliography is also included.

Volunteer Urban Consulting Group. Final Report of the Women's Business Program. New York: Volunteer Urban Consulting Group, 1980. (NTIS Accession No.: PB81-133738.

Through the Office of Special Projects of the Economic Development Administration, the Volunteer Urban Consulting Group (a program of the Harvard Business School Club of New York City) was funded to assist women business owners in socially and economically disadvantaged neighborhoods with management and technical problems. The report is a final summary covering the results of 12 months of work in this area.

The Group used banks, the Small Business Administration, and professional associations to contact women business owners. Over 600 were contacted, but little interest was shown in the program. Management and technical assistance was provided to only 22 women in 1980. The women contacted evidenced needs similar to those of minority business owners, but they also needed better background in basic business understanding and approach.

Women's Development Corporation. <u>Establishment of a Women's Entrepreneurial and Job Development Program</u>. Office of Special Projects, Economic Development Administration, U.S. Department of Commerce, 1980.

The report documents the establishment and first year's operation of the Women's Development Corporation's innovative economic development program. The program was designed to address the particular needs of women who are single or heads of households, to provide opportunities for economic improvement and to create new jobs and enterprises in the greater Providence, Rhode Island area, with a particular focus on the revitalization of Broad Street. The women's entrepreneurial and job development program was part of the Women's Development Corporation's demonstration project to benefit economically disadvantaged, particularly minority women. Minorities participating in the program included black, Hispanic and Asian women.

The program was designed to help women assume greater control over their economic lives--to facilitate equal opportunity for disadvantaged women in response to their particular needs. The program, funded by the Office of Special Projects of the Economic Development Administration, was linked to a housing development program with related support services funded by the Community Services Administration. Activites include: vocational training, business workshops, technical assistance to small businesses and cooperatives, and feasibility studies for building renovation. During the first year of the program, 275 women registered in the entrepreneurial and job assistance program.

The report includes background on neighborhood revitalization in the Elmwood area where the program was centered. Photos and newspaper clippings are also included.

Women's Economic Development Corporation. <u>WEDCO</u>. Quarterly Newsletter of the Women's Economic Development Corporation. St. Paul, Minnesota: 1985.

This quarterly newsletter reports on activities of the Women's Economic Development Corporation (WEDCO) in Minnesota. It describes the type and number of businesses assisted in the first 15 months of the organization's existence, announces new program initiatives, and profiles some of the client businesses assisted. Two management assistance workbooks published by WEDCO are briefly described. Further information on the organization may be obtained from: WEDCO, Iris Park Place, Suite 395, 1885 University Avenue West, St. Paul, Minnesota, 55104.

Selected Guides for Women Business Owners

Gumpert, David E. and Jeffrey A. Timmons. The Insider's Guide to Small Business Resources. New York: Doubleday, 1982.

A wealth of information for the small business person or would-be entrepreneur. The book gives information on education and training, management assistance, federal, state and local government assistance, finance and capital access, franchising, government procurement, exporting for small business; and small business lobbying and service organizations.

There is one chapter on assistance for minority businesses and one chapter on assistance for women. The chapter dealing with women includes information on government assistance, organizations of women business owners and a bibliography.

Jessup, Claudia and Genie Chipps. The Woman's Guide To Starting a Business, rev. ed. New York: Holt, Rinehart and Winston, 1980.

Part 1 is an excellent, thorough guide for the would-be woman business owner. Part 2 profiles 29 women-owned businesses in an interview format written mostly for an audience of women interested in these lines of business. The emphasis is on avoiding the pitfalls of certain types of businesses. The interviews are categorized by the type of business -- most are service and retail-related but some manufacturing firms are included.

McCaslin, Barbara S. and Patricia McNamara. Be Your Own Boss: A Woman's Guide to Planning and Running Her Business. Englewood Cliffs, N.J.: Prentice-Hall, 1980.

A business guide by the two researchers who worked on the California Women Business Owners study. The book has chapters on marketing, legal structure, business start-up, finance, purchasing and inventory, and employee relations Could be very useful for training sessions for prospective business owners. Contains worksheets and answer key.

McVicar, Marjorie. Minding My Own Business: Entrepreneurial Women Share Their Secrets for Success. New York: R. Marek, 1981.

Through interviews with over a hundred women business owners at all life stages and family circumstances, the authors have compiled a practical guide for aspiring women entrepreneurs. The book is divided into two sections. Section 1 provides information on how to set the groundwork for starting a business, i.e, personal analysis, idea development, the development of a business plan, and financing. Section 2 gives specific information on the operation of different types of businesses--retail, service and manufacturing.

Taylor, Charlotte. Women and the Business Game: Strategies for Successful Ownership. New York: Cornerstone Library, 1980.

This thoroughly researched guide for the woman entrepreneur gives some background information on characteristics of women entrepreneurs and problems they face. It discusses first-time entry into business, partnerships, finance, marketing, management and personnel. It also provides lists of private and government agencies that assist women business owners.

This book is more comprehensive than most popular guides. It would be of interest to the academic as well as the woman business owner. It provides background information, discusses the President's Task Force and American Management Association study results, and gives a great deal of anecdotal information on women business owners. Various women business owners were interviewed for the book and brief biographies are included. A bibliography of general business topics is included.

Winston, Sandra. The Entepreneurial Woman. New York: Newsweek Books, 1979.

An informal guide with anecdotal information that might be helpful as general background on the problems women business owners face. Includes a bibliography.

Wisely, Rae. The Independent Woman: How To Start and Succeed In Your Own Business. Los Angeles: J.P. Tarcher, Boston: Distributed by Houghton Mifflin, 1981.

The subtitle of this book, "How to Start and Succeed in Your Own Business," defines its focus. In addition to chapters on business consultants, record keeping, business planning, personnel, advertising and personal issues, it contains a chapter on successful women business owners. Profiles of 12 women-owned businesses are included with special emphasis on the factors that led to their success.

Guides for Home-Based Businesses

Behr, Marion and Wendy Lazar. Women Working Home: The Home-Based Business Guide and Directory. New Jersey: WWH Press, 1981.

Described as a first attempt to discover, identify and assist women who are pursuing gainful work in their homes, this illustrated guide offers practical advice and profiles of women owners of home-based businesses by the founders of the National Alliance of Home-Based Businesswomen. According to the authors, "the book is intended to encourage and aid women who work at home and obtain for them the recognition due an economically useful and socially desirable mode of employment."

Information for the book was collected from several hundred women who filled out questionnaires and wrote letters defining and describing their occupations. As the title suggests, a directory of home-based women-owned businesses in different states is provided.

Delany, George and Sandra. The #1 Home Business Book. Cockeysville, MD: Liberty Publishing Co., 1981.

The book opens with a discussion of successful self-made entrepreneurs and their experiences. It provides information on home business start-up, government regulations and taxes, marketing, and personnel management. The second half of the book is a catalog of 400 ideas for businesses to start at home--everything from auto repair to small-scale light manufacturing.

Feldstein, Stuart. Home, Inc.: How to Start and Operate a Successful Business from Your Home. New York: Grosset and Dunlap, 1981.

Part 1 of this book concentrates mainly on ways to start a home-based enterprise: how to change family relations successfully when more time is spent at home; how to handle taxes, company structure and government regulation; and how to perform home-based marketing. Part 2 is primarily the story of how others run their home operations, in 10 different categories of activity.

Hewes, Jeremy and Joan. Worksteads: Living and Working in the Same Place. San Francisco: The Headlands Press, Inc., 1981.

The authors have labeled this a documentary book. It provides information about home-based careers based on interviews with people who earn their livings at home. The authors believe the significance of the workstead concept (joining the terms for "livelihood" and "surroundings") goes beyond the physical joining of home and workplace, emphasizing a scale of activity that gives equal importance to a person's occupation and to the essential people and comforts of his or her life.

The history of the development of worksteads, the philosophy behind them, the motivations of women and men who operate them, and the legal and tax issues and problems owners face are all discussed at length. Numerous photographs appear, interspersed with profiles of owners and their businesses.

Tepper, Terry P. and Nona Dawe Tepper. The New Entrepreneurs: Women Working From Home. New York: Universe Books, 1980.

This book is a composite of 40 personal narratives and documentary portraits of women throughout the United States who operate businesses from their homes.

Appendix A:
Selected Additional References

I: The Social and Economic Context of Women's Business Ownership

Family Business

Alcorn, Pat B. Success and Survival in the Family-Owned Business. New York: McGraw-Hill, 1982

This book discusses family-owned business issues in an anecdotal manner, and includes treatment of succession and continuity in the family business, as well as family conflicts that emerge over the business or as a result of business activities.

Women's role in the family business is discussed almost exclusively as that of a secondary help-mate, rarely as the principal. Most of the discussion of succession in the family-owned business does not even consider the possibility of a daughter taking over the business. In the preface the author explains that the emphasis on male-dominated business is not intended to deprecate the role of women, but is a "reflection of the subordinate role of women in the vast majority of family businesses."

Carole Sturgis Associates. Women in the Family-Owned Business. Report prepared for the U.S. Small Business Administration, Office of Women's Business Ownership. Washington, D.C.: August 1983.

The subjects for this study were selected from a 4-county metropolitan area in the Midwest. Fifteen people, representing eight family-owned small businesses were interviewed. The precise method of sample selection is not reported. The topics discussed include the general perception of the role of women in the family and in the business, attitudes toward male and female competitiveness and aggressiveness, requirements for establishing a family business and family values and career choice for men and women. Responses focused on difficulties of juggling career and family responsibilities for women, and the need for persistence and support from male family members for women to be involved in family business leadership.

Perhaps due to the heavy reliance on open-ended questions and the relatively unstructured character of the interviews, the study is largely inconclusive.

Danco, Kathy. From the Other Side of the Bed: A Women Looks at Life in the Family Business. Introduction by Leon A. Danco. Cleveland, Ohio: The Center for Family Business, University Press, 1981.

This is one of the few books on the family business written from a woman's perspective. Nevertheless, it focuses almost exclusively on the woman as help-mate to "the Boss," her husband. The book offers tips for the wife on how to understand his problems and how to help out; in short, how to play the role of the boss's wife. Speaking about her own involvement in the family business, the author remarks, "we always managed--by talking--to translate 'his' hopes and dreams into 'ours'."

One chapter, entitled, "Mom Can Own It Too," deals with women as owners-successors in the family-owned business--inheritance by the widow or daughter, and the daughter whose husband takes over control of the business while she retains ownership. The author reports that students in the family business succession seminars put on by herself and her husband are now nearly one-half female, a major change from the time, fairly recently, when the enrollment was 99 percent male.

Dunhill, Mary. Our Family Business. London: Bodley Head, 1979.

A personal reflection on her life, her business and the times in which she lived, by Mary Dunhill, daughter of the founder of the Dunhill Tobacco Company and chair of the board of that company from 1961 to 1976. The book reviews the history of the family business, founded in 1900, the father's background, and gives a description of Ms. Dunhill's experiences as head of the company. The author remarks, "I have tried to illustrate the sort of contribution a woman can make in management, especially in the inter-play of personalities."

Lyman, Amy, Matilde Salganicoff and Barbara Hollandes. "Women in Family Business: An Untapped Resource." Advanced Management Journal 50, 1 (Winter 1984): 46-49

This article discusses the recent rise in the number of women assuming leadership in family business succession. The authors argue that networking, skill evaluation and career planning will help women assume these roles. They conclude that the tendency of family-owned businesses to fail after the first generation could be reversed if the potential of the women in the family were fully developed.

"When Wives Run the Family Business." Business Week (January 17, 1983): 121.

This article discusses the interrelationship between marriages and family-owned businesses, focusing on businesses in which the wife holds the top job. In such cases, men are more willing to let women take the pressure demanded of a leadership role than they used to be, the woman is recognized as the better suited for the job, or she owned the company before her marriage. However, when the wife runs the family business, it can put additional stress on the husband's ego. According to the article, problems can be avoided if the partners establish specific separate territories and clearly indicate who is boss to the employees.

The Socialization of Women

Astin, Helen S., ed., with Allison Parelman and Anne Fisher. Sex Roles: A Research Bibliography. Washington, D.C.: U.S. Department of Health, Education and Welfare, 1975.

Bernard, Jessie. The Female World. New York: The Free Press, 1981.

Davis, Mary Lee. Women In the Traditional Role and Unusual Occupations. Women in American Life series, Book 8. Minneapolis: T.S. Denison, 1976.

Frieze, Irene H., et. al. Women and Sex Roles: A Social Psychological Perspective. New York: Norton, 1978.

Lipman-Blumen, Jean. "Changing Sex Roles in American Culture: Future Directions for Research." Archives of Sexual Behavior 4, 4 (1975): 433-466.

_____. Sex, Gender and Power. Englewood Cliffs, NJ: Prentice Hall, 1983.

Lipman-Blumen, Jean and Ann R. Tickmyer. "Sex Roles in Transition: A Ten Year Perspective." Annual Review of Sociology 1 (1975).

Maccoby, E.M. and C.N. Jacklin. The Psychology of Sex Differences. Stanford, CA: Stanford University Press, 1974.

Murphy, Cullen. "A Survey of the Research." Wilson Quarterly (Winter 1982): 63-80.

Safilios-Rothschild, C. Sex Role Socialization and Sex Discrimination: A Synthesis and Critique of the Literature. Washington, D.C.: National Institute for Education, U.S. Department of Health, Education and Welfare, October, 1979.

Women in the Labor Force

Baden, Clifford. Work and Family: An Annotated Bibliography, 1978-1980. Boston, MA: Wheelock College Center for Parenting Studies, 1981.

Barrett, Nancy S. "Obstacles to Economic Parity for Women." American Economic Review 68, 2 (May 1982): 160-165

Bergmann, B.R. "The Economic Risks of Being A Housewife." American Economic Review (May 1981): 81-86.

Blaxall, M. and B. Reagan, eds. Women and Workplace: The Implications of Occupational Segregation. Chicago: University of Chicago Press, 1976.

Cahn, Ann Foote, ed. Women in the U.S. Labor Force. Foreword by Muriel Humphrey, Introduction by Joan Huber. New York: Praeger, 1979.

Chapman, Jane Roberts, ed. Economic Independence for Women. Beverly Hills: Sage Publications, 1976.

"Exchange: The Theory of Human Capital and the Earnings of Women." Journal of Human Resources 13 (Winter 1979): 103-134.

Fuchs, Victor R. His and Hers: Gender Differences in Work and Income, 1959-1979 (Working Paper, Number 1501). Cambridge, MA: National Bureau of Economic Research, November 1984.

Gealy, Jennifer, Laurie Larwood and Marsha P. Elliott. "Where Sex Counts--Effects of Consultant and Client Gender." Group and Organization Studies 4,2 (June 1979): 201-211.

Hannan, M.T. "Families, Markets and Social Structures." Journal of Economic Literature 701 (March 1982): 65-72.

Kahn-Hut, Rachel, Arlene Kaplan Daniels and Richard Colvard, eds. Women and Work: Problems and Perspectives. New York: Oxford University Press, 1982.

Kahne, H. "Economic Perspectives on the Roles of Women in the American Economy." Journal of Economic Literature 13,4 (December 1975): 249-1292.

Koba Associates, Inc. Women in Non-Traditional Occupations: A Bibliography. Washington, D.C.: U.S. Department of Health, Education and Welfare, 1976.

Larwood, Laurie, and Barbara A. Gutek. "Women at Work in the USA." In Working Women: An International Survey ed. M. J. Davidson and C. L. Cooper. Chichester, U.K.: John Wiley & Sons, 1984.

Larwood, Laurie, and Urs E. Gattiker. "Rational Bias and Interorganizational Power in the Employment of Management Consultants." Group and Organization Studies 10, 1 (March, 1985): 3-10.

Lloyd, C.B. and B.T. Niemi. The Economics of Sex Differentials. New York: Columbia University Press, 1979.

Nieva, Veronica, and Barbara Gutek. Women and Work: A Psychological Perspective. New York: Praeger, 1981.

Norwood, Janet. The Female-Male Earnings Gap: A Review of Employment and Earning Issues. (Report No. 673). Washington, D.C.: U.S. Department of Labor, Bureau of Labor Statistics, 1982.

Norwood, Janet Lippe, and Elizabeth Wallman. Women in the Labor Force: Some New Data Series. (Report No. 673). Washington, D.C.: Department of Labor, Bureau of Labor Statistics, 1982.

Ohio State University, Center for Human Resource Research. Longitudinal Study of the Educational and Labor Market Experience of Young Women: Vol. 4: Years for Decision. R & D Monograph 24. Washington, D.C.: U.S. Department of Labor, Employment and Training Administration, 1978.

Polacheck, S.W. "Occupational Self-Selection: A Human Capital Approach to Sex Differences in Occupational Structure." Review of Economics and Statistics 63 (February 1981): 60-69.

Rytina, N. F. "Occupational Segregation and Earnings Differences by Sex." Monthly Labor Review 104 (January 1981): 49-53.

Smith, R.E., ed. The Subtle Revolution: Women at Work. Washington, D.C.: The Urban Institute, 1979.

_____. Women in the Labor Force in 1990. Washington, D.C.: Urban Institute, 1979.

Treiman, Donald, and Heide Hartmann, eds. Women, Work and Wages: Equal Pay for Jobs of Equal Value. Washington, D.C.: National Academy Press, 1981.

U.S. Department of Labor. U.S. Working Women: A Data Book, Bulletin 1977. Washington, D.C.: U.S. Government Printing Office, 1977.

_____. Women and Work. Washington, D.C.: U.S. Government Printing Office, 1977.

Wallace, Phyllis A. Black Women in the Labor Force. Cambridge, MA: MIT Press, 1980.

Women in Management

Falconer, Merry. "Women in the Executive Suite." Association Management 33 (July 1981): 37-39.

Harrigan, K. R. "Numbers and Positions of Women Elected to Corporate Boards." Academy of Management Journal 24 (September 1981): 619-625.

Hartman, H. "Managers and Entrepreneurs: A Useful Distinction." Administration Science Quarterly 3 (March 1959): 429-451.

Hennig, Margaret, and Anne Jardim. The Managerial Woman. Garden City, N.Y.: Anchor Press/Doubleday, 1977.

Human Resources Corporation. Profile Analysis of Corporate Board Women and Their Corporations: Summary of the Report. San Francisco: 1981.

Kanter, Rosabeth Moss. Men and Women of the Corporation. New York: Basic Books, 1977.

Larwood, Laurie, and Marion Wood. Women in Management. Lexington, Mass: Lexington Books, 1977.

Leavitt, Judith A. Women in Management: 1970-1979, A Bibliography. Chicago: Council of Planning Librarians, 1980. (Council of Planning Librarians Bibliography No. 35).

_____. Women in Management: An Annotated Bibliography and Source List. Phoenix, AZ: Cryx Press, 1982.

Lipman-Blumen, Jean. "Female Leadership in Formal Organizations: Must the Female Leader Go Formal?" In Readings in Managerial Psychology (3rd. ed.) ed. by Harold Leavitt, et al. Chicago: University of Chicago Press, 1980.

Moore, J.M. and A.U. Rickel. "Characteristics of Women in Traditional and Non-Traditional Management Roles." Personnel Psychology 33 (Summer 1982): 319-333.

Schwartz, Eleanor Brantley. The Sex Barrier in Business. Atlanta: Georgia State University, 1971.

Terborg, James R., et al. "Organizational and Personal Correlates of Attitudes Toward Women As Managers." Academy of Management Journal 20 (March 1977): 89-100.

Terborg, James R. "Women in Management: A Research Review." Journal of Applied Psychology (1977): 647-664.

U.S. Department of Labor, Office of the Assistant Secretary for Administration. Women in Management: Selected Recent References. Washington, D.C.: U.S. Government Printing Office, 1978.

Williams, Martha, June Oliver and Meg Gerrard. Women in Management: A Selected Bibliography. (Human Services Monograph Series). Austin: Center for Social Work Research, School of Social Work, University of Texas at Austin, 1977.

Women's Bureau. Women in Management. Washington, D.C.: U.S. Department of Labor, 1980.

II: Entrepreneurship and Small Business Research

Baumback, Clifford M. and Joseph R. Mancuso. Entrepreneurship and Venture Management. Englewood Cliffs, NJ: Prentice-Hall, 1975.

Baumol, William J. "Entrepreneurship in Economic Theory." The American Economic Review 58 (May 1968).

Brockhaus, R.H. "The Effect of Job Dissatisfaction on the Decision to Start A Business." Journal of Small Business Management 18 (January 1980).

_____. "Risk Taking Propensity of Entrepreneurs." Academy of Management Journal 23 (September 1980): 509-520.

_____. "Psychological and Environmental Factors Which Distinquish the Successful from the Unsuccessful Entrepreneur: A Longitudinal Study." Academy of Management Proceedings. Detroit, MI: 1980.

Collins, Orvis F. and David G. Moore. The Organization Makers: A Behavorial Study of Independent Entrepreneurs. New York: Meredith, 1970.

Deeks, J. The Small Firm Owner-Manager: Entrepreneurial Behavior and Management Practice. New York: Praeger, 1976.

Entrepreneurship: Bibliography Series Number 51. Columbus, OH: The National Center For Research in Vocational Education, 1982.

Hornaday, J.A. and J. Aboud. "Characteristics of Successful Entrepreneurs." Personnel Psychology 24 (Summer 1971): 141-153.

Kent, Calvin, Donald Sexton and Sharon Conrad. "Lifetime Experiences of Entrepreneurs: Preliminary Analysis." In Entrepreneurship Education 1981, ed. by Donald Sexton and Philip Van Auken. Waco, TX: Baylor University, Hankamer School of Business, 1981.

Kent, Calvin A., Donald Sexton and Karl Vesper, eds. Encyclopedia of Entrepreneurship. Englewood Cliffs, N.J.: Prentice-Hall, 1982.

McClelland, David C. The Achieving Society. Princeton: D. Van Nostrand, 1961.

Ronen, Joshua, ed. Entrepreneurship. Lexington, MA: D.C. Heath and Co. (Lexington Books), 1983.

Sexton, Donald and R. Smilor eds. The Art and Science of Entrepreneurship. Cambridge, MA: Ballinger, 1985.

Shapero, A. Some Social Dimensions of Entrepreneurship. Working Papers Series: No. WPS 80-69. Columbus, OH: The Ohio State University, College of Administrative Science, August 1980.

Smilor, R. and R.L. Kuhn, eds. Innovations in Business: Take-Off Companies and the Entrepreneurial Spirit. New York: Praeger, 1985.

Timmons, J.S. "Characteristics and Role Demands of Entrepreneurship." American Journal of Small Business 3 (1978): 5-7.

Timmons, Jeffrey A., Leonard E. Smollen and Alexander Dingee. New Venture Creation. Homewood, IL: Richard D. Irwin, 1981.

U.S. Small Business Administration, Office of Advocacy. The Study of Small Business. Washington, DC: U.S. Small Business Administration, 1977. (NTIS #PB-282 7U/1SL).

Weinrauch, J.D. "The Second Time Around: Entrepreneurship as a Mid-Life Alternative." Journal of Small Business Management 18 (January 1980): 25-33.

Zalezuik, A. and M. DeVries. "What Makes Entrepreneurs Entrepreneurial." Business and Society 17 (Spring 1976): 18-23.

Appendix B: Statistics

I: Comparison of Data Sources: 1972-1985

Table I: *Comparison of Three Data Sources on Women Business Owners and Their Firms*

Year	Women-Owned Businesses[1]		Non-Farm Female-Operated Sole Proprietorships[2]		Non-Agricultural Self-Employed Women[3]	
	Total (1000s)	Percent of all	Total (1000s)	Percent of all	Total (1000s)	Percent of all
1972	402	4.6	N.A.	N.A.	1,372	20.7
1977	702	7.1	1,901	22.6	1,692	27.6
1979	N.A.	N.A.	2,341	25.0	1,982	29.1
1980	N.A.	N.A.	2,535	26.0	2,097	29.9
1981	N.A.	N.A.	N.A.	N.A.	2,192	30.8
1982	N.A.	N.A.	2,942	26.0	2,309	31.8
1983	N.A.	N.A.	3,254	27.6	2,439	32.2
1984	N.A.	N.A.	N.A.	N.A.	2,566	33.0
1985	N.A.	N.A.	N.A.	N.A.	2,603	33.4

Sources:
1) *U.S. Bureau of Census. Women-Owned Businesses, 1977.* (Washington, D.C.: U.S. GPO, 1980.)
2) U.S. Department of Treasury, Internal Revenue Service. *Statistics of Income: Sole Proprietorship Returns.* (Washington, D.C.: U.S. GPO. various years).
3) U.S. Bureau of Labor Statistics, *Employment and Earnings,* various issues.

N.A. — not available

II: Sole Proprietorship

Table IIA: *Female-Operated Nonfarm Sole Proprietorships by Industry Division, 1977, 1979, 1980 and 1982 (Thousands)*

Industry Division	Total Nonfarm Sole Proprietorships				Female-Operated Nonfarm Sole Proprietorships			
	1977	1979	1980	1982	1977	1979	1980	1982
All Nonfarm	**8,413.8**	**9,343.6**	**9,730.0**	**10,105.3**	**1,900.7**	**2,341.4**	**2,535.2**	**2,649.3**
Agricultural Services, Forestry and Fishing	245.4	276.2	307.7	293.9	19.5	26.1	30.8	42.1
Mining	71.2	97.5	119.8	138.3	6.1	11.0	11.0	15.5
Construction	994.1	1,097.4	1,073.3	1,202.9	16.1	21.1	19.9	34.7
Transportation, Communications, Electric, Gas and Sanitary Services	385.3	415.5	438.8	451.5	23.6	26.4	27.7	31.1
Wholesale and Retail Trade	2,264.8	2,454.7	2,527.1	2,486.6	641.1	753.4	824.8	840.0
Wholesale	307.2	314.7	329.8	277.0	27.2	31.7	34.0	35.5
Retail	1,862.4	1,985.8	2,066.3	2,123.2	594.4	691.2	759.0	782.3
Unallocated	95.2	154.2	131.1	86.4	19.5	30.5	31.8	22.2
Finance, Insurance & Real Estate	894.9	1,057.7	1,049.0	926.2	225.6	346.0	354.8	294.0
Services	3,302.5	3,654.0	3,842.8	4,275.4	936.6	1,114.6	1,199.7	1,325.3
Non Allocable by Industry	31.4	55.0	75.4	81.5	6.6	12.6	13.2	14.9

Note: Detail may not add to total because of rounding.

Sources: U.S. Department of the Treasury, Internal Revenue Service, *1977 Sole Proprietorship Returns* (Washington, D.C.: Government Printing Office, 1981), Table 1.8; *idem, 1979-1980 Sole Proprietorship Returns* (Washington, D.C.: Government Printing Office, 1982), Table 13, and special tabulation Table 9A, "Nonfarm Sole Proprietorships: Business Receipts and Net Income by Sex of Proprietor and Industry," 1982.

Table IIB: *Amount, Growth, and Share of Business Receipts of Female-Operated Nonfarm Sole Proprietorships by Industry Division, 1977, 1980, and 1982*

Industry Division	Business Receipts (Millions of Dollars)			Annual Percent Growth[1] 1977-1982	Percent of Female-Operated Total		
	1977	1980	1982		1977	1980	1982
Female-Operated Nonfarm Total	**25,176**	**36,377**	**41,717**	**10.6**	**100.0**	**100.0**	**100.0**
Agricultural Services, Forestry and Fishing	153	234	605	31.6	0.6	0.6	1.4
Mining	259	454	917	28.8	1.0	1.2	2.2
Construction	383	682	1,470	30.9	1.5	1.9	3.5
Manufacturing	487	842	1,071	17.1	1.9	2.3	2.5
Transportation, Communications, Electric, Gas, and Sanitary Services	643	698	834	5.3	2.6	1.9	2.0
Wholesale and Retail Trade	13,373	18,938	19,014	7.3	53.1	52.1	45.6
Wholesale	1,378	2,077	937	7.4	5.5	5.7	2.2
Retail	11,752	16,209	17,463	8.2	46.6	44.6	41.9
Unallocated	243	652	614	—	1.0	1.8	1.5
Finance, Insurance & Real Estate	2,258	3,640	3,340	8.2	9.0	10.0	8.0
Services	7,570	10,796	14,359	13.7	30.1	29.7	34.4
Not Allocable by Industry	50	93	108	—	0.2	0.3	0.3

[1] Compound growth rate.

Note: Detail may not add to total because of rounding.

Sources: U.S. Department of the Treasury, Internal Revenue Service, *1977 Sole Proprietorship Returns* (Washington, D.C.: Government Printing Office, 1981), Table 1.8; *idem, 1979-1980 Sole Proprietorship Returns* (Washington, D.C.: Government Printing Office, 1982), Table 13, and special tabulation Table 9A, "Nonfarm Sole Proprietorships: Business Receipts and Net Income by Sex of Proprietor and Industry," 1982.

Table IIC: *Comparison of Average Receipts and Net Income of Sole Proprietorships Operated by Males and Females, 1980*
(Numbers in Dollars)

	Male-Operated		Female-Operated	
	Average Receipts	Average Net Income	Average Receipts	Average Net Income
All Non-farm Industries	53,039	7,139	14,348	2,200
Agricultural Services, Forestry and Fishing	22,535	3,196	7,604	640
Mining	75,328	2,068	41,321	5,975
Construction	44,613	7,054	34,241	3,242
Manufacturing	58,196	6,859	15,784	1,168
Transportation and Public Utilities	47,043	4,850	25,207	1,732
Wholesale and Retail Trades	113,565	5,662	22,961	647
Wholesale	139,861	10,563	61,136	3,526
Retail	111,866	4,494	21,354	497
Unallocated	53,949	5,641	20,525	1,163
Finance, Insurance and Real Estate	26,421	7,688	10,260	4,202
Services	29,495	8,967	8,998	2,756
Personal	20,992	4,868	8,898	2,671
Business	20,554	5,991	8,365	2,806
Automobile Repair & Service	42,310	4,645	38,209	2,519
Miscellaneous Repair	23,432	4,857	16,621	2,808
Medical and Health Services	69,251	30,921	16,128	7,078

Source: Derived from Table 13 of the Department of the Treasury, Internal Revenue Service, *1979-1980 Sole Proprietorship Returns* (Washington, D.C.: U.S. Government Printing Office, 1982).

Table IID: *Number of Sole Proprietors Per 1,000 Persons of Entrepreneurial Age, 1977-1982*

Year	Sole Proprietorships (Thousands) Total	Sole Proprietorships (Thousands) Female-Operated	Resident Population of Entrepreneurial Age (Thousands) Total	Resident Population of Entrepreneurial Age (Thousands) Female	Sole Proprietors Per 1,000 Persons of Entrepreneurial Age (Number) Total	Sole Proprietors Per 1,000 Persons of Entrepreneurial Age (Number) Female
1982	11,170[1]	2,942[1]	176,755	92,258	63	32
1981	10,545	2,780	174,496	91,092	60	31
1980	9,730	2,535	171,954	89,794	57	28
1979	9,344	2,341	168,953	88,238	55	27
1978	8,908	NA	165,932	86,659	54	—
1977	8,414	1,901	162,898	85,056	52	22

Note: NA = Not Available.

[1] The number of sole proprietorships in this table exceeds the number for 1982 in industry tables of the text. The Internal Revenue Service used a count of tax returns rather than business activities for the industry detail to improve estimates of business receipts and net income of sole proprietorships.

Source: U.S. Department of Commerce, Bureau of the Census, *Preliminary Estimates of the Population of the United States by Age, Sex and Race: 1970 to 1981* (Washington, D.C.: Government Printing Office, 1982), Table 2; *idem, Estimates of the Population of the United States by Age, Sex and Race; 1980 to 1983* (Washington, D.C.: Government Printing Office, 1984), Table 2; and U.S. Department of the Treasury, Internal Revenue Service, *1977 Sole Proprietorship Returns* (Washington, D.C.: Government Printing Office, 1981), Table 1.8; *idem, 1979-1980 Sole Proprietorship Returns* (Washington, D.C.: Government Printing Office, 1982), Table 13; special tabulation Table K-3, "Nonfarm Sole Proprietorship Businesses: Business Receipts and Net Income by Sex of Proprietor, Major Industry and by State, Tax Year 1981"; and *idem,* "Tax Year 1982."

III: Self-Employment

Table IIIA: *Comparison of Self-Employed Workers in Non-agricultural Industries By Sex, 1972-1985*

Year	Total (Numbers in thous.)	Male (Percent of yearly totals)	Female (Percent of yearly totals)
1985	7,811	66.6	33.4
1984	7,785	67.0	33.0
1983	7,575	67.8	32.2
1982	7,262	68.2	31.8
1981	7,097	69.1	30.9
1980	7,002	70.1	29.9
1979	6,791	70.8	29.2
1978	6,429	71.8	28.2
1977	6,114	72.3	27.6
1976	5,783	73.2	26.8
1975	5,705	74.0	25.9
1974	5,697	74.1	25.9
1973	5,474	74.1	25.9
1972	5,365	74.4	26.6

Note: Detail may not add to totals because of rounding of data.

Source: U.S. Department of Labor, Bureau of Labor Statistics, Bulletin 2096: *Labor Force Statistics Derived from the Current Population Survey: A Databook,* (September 1982) I: 615-31, Table B-16; *Employment & Earnings,* Household Data, .Annual Averages.

Table IIIB: *Self-Employed Workers in Non-Agricultural Industries by Sex, 1985*

Industry	Male (1,000)	Percent of all Self-employed Males	Female (1,000)	Percent of All Self-employed Females
Mining	19	0.5	1	0.04
Construction	1,244	22.4	57	2.20
Manufacturing	260	5.7	88	3.40
Transportation & Public Utilities	273	5.4	42	1.60
Wholesale & Retail Trade	1,084	23.0	709	27.00
Finance, Insurance & Real Estate	373	6.6	186	7.00
Services	1,955	35.5	1,522	58.40
TOTAL	5,208	100.0	2,605	100.00

Note: Detail may not add to totals because of rounding of data.

Source: *Employment and Earnings,* U.S. Department of Labor, Bureau of Labor Statistics, January, 1986.

Table IIIC: *Earnings of Self-Employed Workers by Sex, 1980 and 1983*

	Number With Earnings (thous.)		Median Earnings (dollars)		Mean Earnings (dollars)	
	1980	1983	1980	1983	1980	1983
MALE						
Year-Round Full-Time	4,212	4,252	12,743	16,031	17,536	20,704
All	6,197	6,482	10,816	11,175	14,589	16,626
FEMALE						
Year-Round Full-Time	820	1,012	5,144	7,715	7,977	10,809
All	2,361	2,756	2,144	2,884	4,673	6,206

Source: *Monthly Income of Households, Families, and Persons in the United States:* 1980.
Current Population Reports: Consumer Income, Series P-60, No. 132 and 146. Washington, D.C.: U.S. Department of Commerce, Bureau of the Census, July 1982, Table 58 and April, 1985, Table 54.

Table IIID: *Characteristics of Self-Employed Workers by Level of Educational Attainment and Sex, 1980*

Educational Attainment	Female					Male				
	Number (Thousands)	Percent	Female Average Age	Average Self-Employment Income (Dollars)	Average Wage-and-Salary Income (Dollars)	Number (Thousands)	Percent	Male Average Age	Average Self-Employment Income (Dollars)	Average Wage-and-Salary Income (Dollars)
Total Self-Employed	**2,453**	**100.0**	**43**	**3,874**	**5,938**	**7,811**	**100.0**	**41**	**10,950**	**13,340**
Less than High School	548	22.3	48	3,129	3,983	2,155	27.6	41	7,506	8,765
High School Graduate	886	36.1	42	3,469	6,231	2,184	28.0	39	10,435	13,763
Started but did not Complete College	601	24.5	36	4,064	6,373	1,518	19.4	35	9,763	13,274
Completed 4 Years of College	25	9.2	41	4,383	8,961	818	10.5	41	12,402	21,581
Completed More Than 4 Years of College	193	7.9	40	6,666	9,897	1,136	14.5	41	19,003	21,803

Source: Unpublished tabulation of self-employment figures for males and females derived from the *1980 Census of Population 1/1,000 sample.* Tabulations from Office of Advocacy, U.S. Small Business Administration, 1984.

IV: Distribution of Federal Contracts to Small Business by Sex of Owner

Table IVA: *Federal Prime Contract Actions Over $10,000 to Small Business and Women-Owned Business, FY 1982-FY 1983*

	Contract Actions over $10,000 (Thousands of Dollars)		Small Business Share (Percent)		Percent Change
	FY 1982	FY 1983	FY 1982	FY 1983	FY 1982-FY 1983
Small Business Actions	23,355,024	21,757,837	100.0	100.0	—6.8
Women-Owned Business Actions	545,467	603,722	2.3	2.8	10.7

Note: From FY 1982 to FY 1983, total Federal Government prime contract actoins of over $10,000 increased from $152.0 billion to $154.2 billion, or by 1.4 percent. The awards to women-owned business were 0.3 percent of the FY 1982 total and 0.4 percent of the FY 1983 total.

Source: Federal Procurement Data Center, Special Report 1226A, July 25, 1984.

Table IVB: *Distribution of Prime Contract Actions Over $10,000 to Small Business and Women-Owned Business by Product or Service Category, FY 1982-FY 1983*

	Women-Owned Business		Small Business	
Product/Service	FY 1982	FY 1983	FY 1982	FY 1983
Total	100.0	100.0	100.0	100.0
Research and Development	4.3	2.9	4.1	4.7
Other Services and Construction	50.9	63.6	41.9	48.6
Supplies and Equipment	44.8	33.5	54.0	46.7

Source: Federal Procurement Data Center, Special Report 1274, August 21, 1984.

V: Small Business Data Base

Table VA: *Number of Nonfarm Enterprises in the Small Business Data Base by Industry Division and Sex of Owner-Operator, 1984*

| Industry Division | Thousands | | | | Percent of Nonfarm Industries | | Female-Operated As Percent of Industry |
	Total	Male-Operated	Female Operated	Male-Female jointly Operated	Total	Female Operated	
All Nonfarm[1]	**5,825**	**3,961**	**551**	**1,313**	**100.0**	**100.0**	**9.5**
Agricultural Services, Forestry, and Fishing	171	106	2	64	2.9	0.3	1.0
Mining	28	18	5	6	0.5	0.9	18.2
Construction	648	480	19	150	11.1	3.4	2.9
Manufacturing	445	359	26	60	7.6	4.8	5.9
Transportation, Communications & Public Utilities	187	111	23	54	3.2	4.2	12.2
Wholesale Trade	545	376	35	133	9.4	6.4	6.5
Retail Trade	1,617	1,017	188	412	27.8	34.1	11.6
Finance, Insurance & Real Estate	529	385	30	113	9.1	5.4	5.7
Services	1,653	1,109	223	321	28.4	40.5	13.5

[1] Totals do not include some establishments that could not be classified by type of industry.

Note: Estimates derived from a sample of the Small Business Data Base Master Establishment List (MEL) of more than 8.1 million establishment and enterprise records. The MEL is created by matching two commercially available sources, the Dun's Market Identifier file from Dun and Bradstreet with the Market Data Retrieval, Inc. file, a "Yellow Pages" telephone listing. Percentages derived from unrounded data.

Source: Small Business Data Base, Ownership Characteristics Survey, Office of Advocacy, U.S. Small Business Administration, 1984.

Appendix C:
Presidential Documents

Reprinted from — **Federal Register** / Vol. 44, No. 100 / Tuesday, May 22, 1979 / Presidential Documents

Presidential Documents

Executive Order 12138 of May 18, 1979

Creating a National Women's Business Enterprise Policy and Prescribing Arrangements for Developing, Coordinating and Implementing a National program for Women's Business Enterprise

In response to the findings of the Interagency Task Force on Women Business Owners and congressional findings that recognize:

1. the significant role which small business and women entrepreneurs can play in promoting full employment and balanced growth in our economy;

2. the many obstacles facing women entrepreneurs; and

3. the need to aid and stimulate women's business enterprise;

By the authority vested in me as President of the United States of America, in order to create a National Women's Business Enterprise Policy and to prescribe arrangements for developing, coordinating and implementing a national program for women's business enterprise, it is ordered as follows:

1—1. *Responsibilities of the Federal Departments and Agencies.*

1—101. Within the constraints of statutory authority and as otherwise permitted by law:

(a) Each department and agency of the Executive Branch shall take appropriate action to facilitate, preserve and strengthen women's business enterprise and to ensure full participation by women in the free enterprise system.

(b) Each department and agency shall take affirmative action in support of women's business enterprise in appropriate programs and activities including but not limited to:

(1) management, technical, financial and procurement assistance.

(2) business-related education, training, counseling and information dissemination, and

(3) procurement.

(c) Each department or agency empowered to extend Federal financial assistance to any program or activity shall issue regulations requiring the recipient of such assistance to take appropriate affirmative action in support of women's business enterprise and to prohibit actions or policies which discriminate against women's business enterprise on the ground of sex. For purposes of this subsection, Federal financial assistance means assistance extended by way of grant, cooperative agreement, loan or contract other than a contract of insurance or guaranty. These regulations shall prescribe sanctions for noncompliance. Unless otherwise specified by law, no agency sanctions shall be applied until the agency or department concerned has advised the appropriate person or persons of the failure to comply with its regulations and has determined that compliance cannot be secured by voluntary means.

1—102. For purposes of the Order, affirmative action may include, but is not limited to, creating or supporting new programs responsive to the special needs of women's business enterprise, establishing incentives to promote business or business-related opportunities for women's business enterprise, collecting and disseminating information in support of women's business enterprise, and insuring to women's business enterprise knowledge of and ready access to business-related services and resources. If, in implementing this Order, an agency undertakes to use or to require compliance with numerical set-asides, or similar measures, it shall state the purpose of such measure, and the measure shall be designed on the basis of pertinent factual findings of discrimination against women's business enterprise and the need for such measure.

1—103. In carrying out their responsibilities under Section 1—1, the departments and agencies shall consult the Department of Justice, and the Department of Justice shall provide leagl guidance concerning these responsibilities.

1—2. *Establishment of the Interagency Committee on Women's Business Enterprise.*

1—201. To help insure that the actions ordered above are carried out in an effective manner, I hereby establish the Interagency Committee on Women's Business Enterprise (hereinafter called the Committee).

1—202. The Chairperson of the Committee (hereinafter called the Chairperson) shall be appointed by the President. The Chairperson shall be the presiding officer of the Committee and shall have such duties as prescribed in this order or by the Committee in its rules of procedure. The Chairperson may also represent his or her department, agency or office on the Committee.

1—203. The Committee shall be composed of the Chairperson and other members appointed by the heads of departments and agencies from among high level policy-making officials. In making these appointments, the recommendations of the Chairperson shall be taken into consideration. The following departments and agencies and such other departments and agencies as the Chairperson shall select shall be members of the Committee: the Departments of Agriculture; Commerce; Defense; Energy; Health, Education, and Welfare; Housing and Urban Development; Interior; Justice; Labor; Transportation; Treasury; the Federal Trade Commission; General Services Administration; National Science Foundation; Office of Federal Procurement Policy; and the Small Business Administration. These members shall have a vote. Nonvoting members shall include the Executive Director of the Committee and at least one but no more than three representatives from the Executive Office of the President appointed by the President.

1—204. The Committee shall meet at least quarterly at the call of the Chairperson, and at such other times as may be determined to be useful according to the rules of procedure adopted by the Committee.

1—205. The Administrator of the Small Business Administration shall provide an Executive Director and adequate staff and administrative support for the Committee. The staff shall be located in the Office of the Chief Counsel for Advocacy of the Small Business Administration, or in such other office as may be established specifically to further the policies expressed herein. Nothing in this Section prohibits the use of other properly available funds and resources in support of the Committee.

1—3. *Functions of the Committee.* The Committee shall in a manner consistent with law:

1—301. Promote, coordinate and monitor the plans, programs and operations of the departments and agencies of the Executive Branch which may contribute to the establishment, preservation and strengthening of women's business enterprise. It may, as appropriate, develop comprehensive interagency plans and specific program goals for women's business enterprise with the cooperation of the departments and agencies.

1—302. Establish such policies, definitions, procedures and guidelines to govern the implementation, interpretation and application of this order, and generally perform such functions and take such steps as the Committee may deem to be necessary or appropriate to achieve the purposes and carry out the provisions hereof.

1—303. Promote the mobilization of activities and resources of State and local governments, business and trade associations, private industry, colleges and universities, foundations, professional organizations, and volunteer and other groups toward the growth of women's business enterprise, and facilitate the coordination of the efforts of these groups with those of the departments and agencies.

1—304. Make an annual assessment of the progress made in the Federal Government toward assisting women's business enterprise to enter the mainstream of business ownership and to provide recommendations for future actions to the President.

1—305. Convene and consult as necessary with persons inside and outside government to develop and promote new ideas concerning the development of women's business enterprise.

1—306. Consider the findings and recommendations of government and private sector investigations and studies of the problems of women entrepreneurs, and promote further research into such problems.

1—307. Design a comprehensive and innovative plan for a joint Federal and private sector effort to develop increased numbers of new women-owned businesses and larger and more successful women-owned businesses. The plan should set specific reasonable targets which can be achieved at reasonable and identifiable costs and should provide for the measurement of progress towards these targets at the end of two and five years. Related outcomes such as income and tax revenues generated, jobs created, new products and services introduced or new domestic or foreign markets created should also be projected and measured in relation to costs wherever possible. The Committee should submit the plan to the President for approval within six months of the effective date of this Order.

1—4 *Other Responsibilities of the Federal Departments and Agencies.*

1—401. The head of each department and agency shall designate a high level official to have the responsibility for the participation and cooperation of that department or agency in carrying out this Executive order. This person may be the same person who is the department or agency's representative to the Committee.

1—402. To the extent permitted by law, each department and agency upon request by the Chairperson shall furnish information, assistance and reports and otherwise cooperate with the Chairperson and the Committee in the performance of their functions hereunder. Each department or agency shall ensure that systematic data collection processes are capable of providing the Committee current data helpful in evaluating and promoting the efforts herein described.

1—403. The officials designated under Section 1—401, when so requested, shall review the policies and programs of the women's business enterprise program and shall keep the Chairperson informed of proposed budget, plans and programs of their departments or agencies affecting women's business enterprise.

1—404. Each Federal department or agency, within constraints of law, shall continue current efforts to foster and promote women's business enterprise and to support the program herein set forth, and shall cooperate with the Chairperson and the Committee in increasing the total Federal effort.

1—5. *Reports.*

1—501. The Chairperson shall, promptly after the close of the fiscal year, submit to the President a full report of the activities of the Committee hereunder during the previous fiscal year. Further, the Chairperson shall, from time to time, submit to the President the Committee's recommendations for legislation or other action to promote the purposes of this Order.

1—502. Each Federal department and agency shall report to the Chairperson as hereinabove provided on a timely basis so that the Chairperson and the Committee can consider such reports for the Committee report to the President.

1—6. *Definitions.* For the purposes of this Order, the following definitions shall apply:

1—601. "Women-owned business" means a business that is at least 51 percent owned by a woman or women who also control and operate it. "Control" in this context means exercising the power to make policy decisions. "Operate"; in this context means being actively involved in the day-to-day management.

1—602. "Women's business enterprise" means a woman-owned business or businesses or the efforts of a woman or women to establish, maintain or develop such a business or businesses.

1—603. Nothing in subsections 1—601 or 1—602 of this Section (1—6) should be construed to prohibit the use of other definitions of a woman-owned business or women's business enterprise by departments and agencies of the Executive Branch where other definitions are deemed reasonable and useful for any purpose not inconsistent with the purposes of this Order. Wherever feasible, departments and agencies should use the definition of a woman-owned business in subsection 1—601 above for monitoring performance with respect to women's business enterprise in order to assure comparability of data throughout the Federal Government.

1—7. *Construction.* Nothing in this order shall be construed as limiting the meaning or effect of any existing Executive Order.

Jimmy Carter

THE WHITE HOUSE.
May 18, 1979.

Federal Register
Vol. 48, No. 124
Monday, June 27, 1983

Presidential Documents

Title 3—

The President

Executive Order 12426 of June 22, 1983

President's Advisory Committee on Women's Business Ownership

By the authority vested in me as President by the Constitution and laws of the United States of America, and in order to establish, in accordance with the provisions of the Federal Advisory Committee Act, as amended (5 U.S.C. App. I), an advisory committee on women's business ownership, it is hereby ordered as follows:

Section 1. *Establishment.* (a) There is established the President's Advisory Committee on Women's Business Ownership. The Committee shall be composed of no more than 15 members appointed or designated by the President. These members shall have particular knowledge and expertise concerning the current status of businesses owned by women in the economy and methods by which these enterprises might be encouraged to expand.

(b) The President shall designate a Chairperson from among the members of the Committee.

Sec. 2. *Functions.* (a) The Committee shall review the status of businesses owned by women; foster, through the private sector, financial, educational, and procurement support for women entrepreneurs; and provide appropriate advice to the President and the Administrator of the Small Business Administration on these issues.

(b) The Committee shall submit reports to the President on a periodic basis.

Sec. 3. *Administration.* (a) The heads of Executive agencies shall, to the extent permitted by law, provide the Committee such information as it may require for purposes of carrying out its functions.

(b) Members of the Committee shall serve without compensation for their work on the Committee. However, members appointed from among private citizens of the United States may, subject to the availability of funds, be allowed travel expenses, including per diem in lieu of subsistence, as authorized by law for persons serving intermittently in the government service (5 U.S.C. 5701-5707).

(c) The Administrator of the Small Business Administration shall, to the extent permitted by law, provide the Committee with such administrative services, funds, facilities, staff and other support services as may be necessary for the performance of its functions.

Sec. 4. *General.* (a) Notwithstanding any other Executive Order, the functions of the President under the Federal Advisory Committee Act, as amended, except that of reporting to the Congress, which are applicable to the Committee, shall be performed by the Administrator of the Small Business Administration, in accordance with guidelines and procedures established by the Administrator of General Services.

(b) The Committee, shall terminate one year from the date of this Order.

[FR Doc. 83-17428
Filed 6-24-83; 10:43 am]
Billing code 3195-01-M

THE WHITE HOUSE,
June 22, 1983.

Ronald Reagan

Editorial Note: The President's remarks of June 22, 1983, on signing Executive Order 12426, are printed in the *Weekly Compilation of Presidential Documents* (vol. 19, no. 25).

Appendix D:
Office of Women's Business Ownership: Purpose and Charter

The Office of Women's Business Ownership, with a consistituency of more than 3 million women business owners, was formed to implement a national policy to support women entrepreneurs. The Director of the Office reports to the Assosociate Deputy Administrator for Special Programs and has the responsibility for insuring that the provisions of Executive Order 12138, and other Administration and Congressional guidance concerning women's business ownership are carried out. The primary functions of the Office of Women's Business Ownership include:

- Develop and coordinate a national program to increase the number and success of women-owned businesses while making maximum use of existing government and private sector resources;

- Develop policy, plans, operating procedures, and standards to effectively strengthen and improve the Agency responsiveness to the needs of current or potential woman business owners;

- Research and evaluate the special programmatic needs of current or potential women business owners and develop and test ways of meeting them;

- Provide support to the Interagency Committee on Women's Business Enterprise in fulfilling its mandate to promote, coordinate, and monitor Federal efforts on behalf of women business owners;

- Work with Federal, state and local governments to insure that they consider women's business ownership in their program areas. Estab- lish and maintain a free flow of information in both directions; and

- Serve as principal liaison with business, educational, philanthropic, organizational, and community resources to assist the growth and development of women-owned businesses.

These responsibilities are carried out with the assistance of eighty-one (81) woman business Coordinators and Representatives located in SBA regional and district offices across the country. The Coordinators and Representatives play a critical role in insuring Agency responsiveness to the concerns of women business owners. For more information, contact:

Office of Women's Business Ownership
U.S. Small Business Administration
1441 L Street, N.W., Room 414
Washington, D.C. 20416
(202) 653-8000

Appendix E:
Index of Authors Names

Treiman, Donald, 144
Trescott, Martha Moore
   Scott, 95

U.S. Commission on Civil
   Rights, 31, 32, 36, 47, 53, 123
U.S. Congress. House. Committee
   on Commerce, Transportation
   & Tourism, 53
U.S. Congress. House. Subcommittee
   on Energy & Commerce, 30, 53
U.S. Congress. House. Committee
   on Small Business, 14, 33, 126, 127
U.S. Congress. Joint Economic Com-
   mittee, 125
U.S. Congress. Senate. Committee
   on Commerce, Science & Trans-
   portation, 54, 55
U.S. Congress. Senate. Committee
   on Finance, SubCommittee on
   Estate & Gift Taxation, 44
U.S. Congress. Senate. Committee
   on the Judiciary. Subcommittee
   on Anti-Trust, Monopoly and
   Business Rights, 54
U.S. Congress. Senate. Committee
   on Labor & Human Resources.
   Subcommittee on Labor, 54
U.S. Congress. Senate. Select
   Committee on Small Business, 33,
   127, 128
U.S. Department of Commerce 124
U.S. Department of Commerce,
   Bureau of the Census, 4, 5, 6, 13,
   19, 20, 22, 27, 33, 38, 111, 112,
   113
U.S. Department of Commerce, Economic
   Development Administration, 23, 129,
   136
U.S. Department of Health, Education
   & Welfare, 19
U.S. Department of Labor, Bureau of
   Labor Statistics, 3, 4, 6, 113, 144
U.S. Department of Labor, Employment
   and Training Administration, 144
U.S. Department of Labor, National
   Commission on the Observance of
   International Women's Year, 32, 33,
   35, 95
U.S. Department of Labor, Office of
   the Assistant Secretary For
   Administration, 145

U.S. Department of Labor, Women's
   Bureau, 145
U.S. Department of Treasury,
   Internal Revenue Service, 3,4,5,111
U.S. Department of Treasury, Study
   Team on Credit & Capital Formation
   Among Women-Owned Businesses, 47, 55,
   118
U.S. Federal Reserve Board, 63, 64, 65
U.S. General Accounting Office, 37, 124
U.S. Interagency Committee on Women's
   Business Enterprise, 96, 124
U.S. Small Business Administration, 2, 3,
   5, 14, 23, 37, 97, 113, 130, 134, 147
U.S. Small Business Administration,
   Office of Women's Business Owner-
   ship, 35, 36, 140

Verble, Sedelta D., 135
Vesper, Karl, 8, 9, 17, 146
View, Janice, 105
Volunteer Urban Consulting Group, 135

Waddell, Frederick Thomass, 12, 109
Wahl, Beverly, 31, 52
Wallace, Phyllis A., 144
Wallman, Elizabeth, 144
Walton, Frances, 135
Warren, Audrey, 17, 93
Webb, Meredith, 36, 120
WEDCO: Women's Economic Development
   Corporation, 24, 136
Weinrauch, J.D., 147
Welsch, Harold, 10, 22, 98, 110
Wetzel, William, 28
White House Conference on Small
   Business, 35, 124, 125
White House Task Force ("50 States
   Project"), 31, 61
White, Jerry, 98
Widerman, Jane, 72
Williams, Constance, 35, 98
Williams, Martha, 145
Williams, Wendy, 30
Winston, Sandra, 138
Wisely, Rae, 138
Women's Rights Law Reporter, 51
Wood, Marion, 145

Young, Earl, 10, 22, 98, 110

Zalezuik, A., 147